**Acknowledgement of Country**

The author gratefully acknowledges the Nyangbul people of the Bundjalung Nation as the Traditional Custodians and original storytellers of the place where she built her tiny house and wrote this book, and pays her respects to all elders past and present of the many nations that make up this country we now call Australia.

**Publisher's note:** Some names and identifying details in this book have been changed to protect the privacy of individuals. Where names have been changed, any likeness to a person of that name is purely coincidental.

Published in 2024 by Hardie Grant Explore, an imprint of Hardie Grant Publishing

Hardie Grant Explore (Melbourne)
Wurundjeri Country
Building 1, 658 Church Street
Richmond, Victoria 3121

Hardie Grant Explore (Sydney)
Gadigal Country
Level 7, 45 Jones Street
Ultimo, NSW 2007

www.hardiegrant.com/au/explore

All rights reserved. No part of this publication may be reproduced, stored in a retrieval system or transmitted in any form by any means, electronic, mechanical, photocopying, recording or otherwise, without the prior written permission of the publishers and copyright holders.

The moral rights of the author have been asserted.

Copyright text and photography © Louise Southerden 2024
Copyright design © Hardie Grant Publishing 2024

 A catalogue record for this book is available from the National Library of Australia

Hardie Grant acknowledges the Traditional Owners of the Country on which we work, the Wurundjeri People of the Kulin Nation and the Gadigal People of the Eora Nation, and recognises their continuing connection to the land, waters and culture. We pay our respects to their Elders past and present.

Tiny: A Memoir About Love, Letting Go and a Very Small House
ISBN 9781741179224

10 9 8 7 6 5 4 3 2 1

Project editor
Megan Cuthbert
Editor
Siboney Saavedra
Proofreader
Helen Koehne
Trainee editor
Olivia Brown
Design
Regine Abos
Typesetting
Michael Kuszla
Production manager
Simone Wall

Colour reproduction by Splitting Image Colour Studio

Printed in Australia by Griffin Press.

 The paper this book is printed on is certified against the Forest Stewardship Council® Standards. Griffin Press – a member of the Opus Group holds chain of custody certification SCS-COC-001185 FSC® promotes environmentally responsible, socially beneficial and economically viable management of the world's forests.

# Tiny

A memoir about love, letting go
and a very small house

by Louise Southerden

**Author's note**

It's almost impossible to write a memoir without mentioning other people, people who (mostly) didn't ask to be written about, so I've changed the names and identifying details of some of them to protect their privacy, and obtained permission from others to include them. I've also tried to be as open, honest and kind as possible about the intimate relationship that ran alongside the story of the tiny build, and remember that there are always reasons for the things we say and do, upstream of our words and actions, often invisible to others, even to ourselves. But love is complicated; I understand and accept that other people might have their own take on what happened. All I can do is share my story, as I experienced it.

*'May your trails be crooked, winding, lonesome, dangerous, leading to the most amazing view... where something strange and more beautiful and more full of wonder than your deepest dreams waits for you.'*
~ Edward Abbey

# Introduction

What does it mean to come home? To know, when you're not there, that you have a place of your own, perhaps just a room, that feels safe in all the important ways? That wraps its arms around you when you arrive at the doorstep drenched in the problems of the world and desperate for peace? A place where you know, in your bones, you belong?

For decades, whenever I thought of home I didn't picture the houses I'd grown up in. Family wasn't synonymous with home for me, either; the two seemed unrelated after a certain point in my life. Instead I thought of places I'd stayed on my travels. Serene hotel rooms, rumbling ships' cabins, hip-swaying compartments on overnight trains. Small spaces that made me feel safely contained and part of something bigger at the same time.

I wanted to create a home like that, one I wouldn't have to fly halfway around the world to find, one that would stay right where I'd left it, so I would always know where I was. I knew it would be difficult to do such a thing, but it turned out to be all kinds of difficult I couldn't have imagined. And when I eventually emerged on the other side, I could see that the destination – a home of my own – had been worth the effort of getting there, though at times I wasn't at all sure it would be.

# Prologue

The cabin was all wood and windows, lumber and light. Perched on top of a hill that appeared to be made entirely of trees, it had walls as dark as chocolate and cherry-red window frames. A small metal chimney poked from its slate roof. I'd been hiking for two hours, the last bit a sweaty, never-ending uphill slog, when the forest trail I'd been following suddenly petered out in a clearing. The air around me brightened and there it was, my little home away from home. I was instantly smitten.

Like so many nature-lovers, I'd long daydreamed about staying in a cabin in the woods for a while, or longer. Just saying the word 'cabin' – even writing it now – always opens up a skylight in my mind and lets in a little peace. A few summers ago, while I was rambling around Europe trying to figure out where to go next in my life and not finding answers, not even knowing which questions to ask, I really wanted, and needed, some of that peace. I also had a vague desire to try out a simple, back-to-nature existence, to find out if I was capable of chopping wood and carrying water and being utterly alone in nature for more than a few days.

Then, trawling online one lazy afternoon, I found this little cabin. It was in southern Norway, had been built by loggers in the 1940s and had recently become a Scout hut; the Scouts now rented it out to travellers when they weren't using it. I silently thanked them – the loggers as well as the Scouts – booked the cabin for as long as my travel funds would allow, and experienced the first rush of aliveness I'd felt in months.

I was still breathing hard when I unlocked the cabin's heavy wooden door and pulled it open. Inside, I dropped my backpack on the dusty wooden floor and surveyed my new abode. The single room, dominated by an ancient wood-burning stove, was the epitome of simplicity and everything I'd hoped for, all at once. A bank of kitchen cabinets slouched against one wall. There was a basic couch and a bunk bed. A wooden table with a bench seat faced a large window that framed a view full of trees; Christmassy pines and firs populated the slopes below while all around the cabin were slender, silvery birch trees that could have sprouted from a fairy tale.

There was no electricity, no running water. No phone reception or internet connection. Candles were provided and I'd brought a head-torch out of habit, but I figured I wouldn't need either; at this time of year, the sun was setting well after my bedtime each night.

Orientation done, I thought: *A cup of tea would be nice.* Then, a realisation: to make tea, one needs water. I'd have to walk to the lake, a downhill kilometre away, to fetch water for the next day or two. The day was warm, so I tossed my swimsuit into a daypack, picked up two plastic jerrycans I'd seen by the door and set off.

At the lake, I changed into my swimsuit – again out of habit, there being no one else around – and lowered myself into the cool water, suddenly noticing how exhausted I was, how anxious I'd felt all day about the prospect of spending two whole weeks alone. I swam across the smooth water, then floated on my back for a while, looking up at a world of sky. My body smiled all over. Back on land, I lay on a smooth rock to dry off in the late afternoon sun before shrugging on my clothes and filling the jerrycans in preparation for the ten-minute walk back to the cabin.

As soon as I started walking, however, I started to lose my bearings. I didn't recognise any of the trees or rocks around me. In all my excitement – *I was staying in a cabin, in Norway!* – I hadn't paid attention to where I was going, or how I was going to get back. Now I was going to perish in the very place I'd fantasised about.

I sat down on a log and suddenly remembered something a Scout leader had once told me (it seemed apt): *In a crisis, Scouts always take action*. I might have been tired, weighed down by two water containers and alone in a totally unfamiliar environment, but I could do *something*. I took a deep breath, reminded myself that darkness was still hours away and there were no bears in these woods (I was almost certain), then studied the hand-drawn map I'd found in the cabin and stuffed in my pocket, just in case. There was a second dotted line on it, marking a longer but more distinct trail than the one I'd taken earlier. I retraced my steps, found the longer trail and eventually spied, through those spindly birch trees, my little cabin. For the second time that day, I was home.

That night, I made a sandwich for dinner and collapsed onto the lower bunk hours before the sun eventually went down. With no phone and no watch and no clock in the cabin, I had no way of knowing what the actual time was, or what time I woke up the next morning – and I loved not knowing, the position of the sun telling me roughly where I was in the day, a truer timepiece than any other.

My days fell into a simple, satisfying routine. The fire was a living thing I coaxed alive every morning with offerings of kindling I'd whittled with my Swiss Army knife and whispered awake with my breath at various times during the day. I watched it, learned to read its rhythms, listened for the tell-tale crackles that told me it was happy. Then I'd boil water for tea and make porridge for breakfast and sit outside to eat and wash the dishes in a basin of water. After that I'd find something useful to do, like mending my clothes, worn from months of constant travel, or cleaning the cabin's windows or splitting logs with an axe.

Without the need to rush, each job could take exactly as long as it took. I didn't need to think about anything else as I worked. There was nowhere I had to be as soon as I was finished. One day an unfamiliar thought came to me: *doing ordinary things with your hands can be immensely calming*.

With my morning chores done and my next meal hours away, I had unlimited, uninterrupted time to read, write, draw and just listen to the birds and the wind rustling the tops of the trees. I collected leaves and stones to decorate the window sills, picked wild strawberries and blueberries to snack on, swam every day and paddled a canoe around the lake. I also had an entire forest to explore – and got lost a few more times, until I started making little pine cone trail-markers for myself.

One evening, I lit a few candles and sat at the table to watch a storm approach from the valley below. The wind howled and my little cabin shook and creaked like an old sailing ship built to withstand anything nature could throw at it, and I had an overwhelming feeling of safety. Another night, I braved the elements to run outside and danced naked in the summer rain.

I didn't once feel lonely, or afraid. I can't remember ever feeling so content.

Towards the end of my stay, I started walking in the forest barefoot. It slowed me down and opened me up to a world of sensations otherwise out of reach: the cool dampness of mud puddles, the tickle of sticks and seeds, the smoothness of rocks that had been warmed by the sun.

When it was time to shoulder my backpack and return to civilisation, I locked the door behind me, took one last look at my cabin. In just two weeks, it had recalibrated me, become my home in some true way. And brought me home to myself. I felt more grounded in my body, in my life, than I had in a long time. More tuned in to the real world, after being unplugged from the human-centric one for a while. Of all the small places I'd stayed in over the years, all the beach shacks and mountain huts and tents and treehouses, this little cabin had had the biggest impact on me, and as I walked away from it, something inside me quietly decided: I want to live like this.

# PART 1
# **BEFORE**

*'To be free is to learn, to test yourself constantly, to gamble. It is not safe.'* ~ Robyn Davidson

Chapter 1

# Lost

If I had to rewind my life to a time when I felt as cosy and content as I had in that cabin in Norway, I'd probably stop at the Sunday my dad built a cubby for eight-year-old me and my little brother, Tim, in the backyard of our suburban Sydney house.

Made of old fence palings – its fourth wall actually was the back fence – the cubby was so small my outstretched arms could touch both sides at the same time. It had tiny stairs leading up to its tiny porch and a single square window hole made pretty with a pair of red gingham curtains. The finishing touch was an empty Sunlight soapbox out the front, the pretend letterbox for our small pretend house.

I remember spending whole weekends in that cubby, messing around, re-arranging the small chairs and a dresser containing tiny cups and saucers, pretending it was a shop or a restaurant, Tim and I taking turns being patron and host.

Our parents sold that family home a couple of years later, to upgrade to one that was bigger, if not better, something they kept doing every few years throughout my childhood and adolescence. I resisted every one of those moves, hated wrenching myself from yet another house I'd come to love, never seemed to learn how to *not* become attached to them. I understood the upwardly mobile times we lived in, the economic sense of moving. And there were probably practical reasons we couldn't have another cubby: nowhere to build one at our next house, perhaps, or it was decided that Tim and I were getting too old for such things.

Still, I was silently devastated to lose that cubby. At the time, I couldn't have said why. Small houses weren't on my radar in any other way; no adult I knew lived in one and I hadn't yet travelled to parts of the world where people do, often by choice. My sense of loss seemed too large for a small playhouse. Maybe because underneath it was another feeling: that I was losing something I'd only just learned was important to me, something I'd one day need to find again.

⌂

Mum was always 'home' to me. Dad was the boss, but Mum was home. Not just because of her sunny nature or her constant physical presence, but because she was the one who listened to my stories, as I sat at the kitchen counter after school with a mug of Milo and a piece of cake still warm from the oven. The one who remembered the smallest details of my friends' lives, laughed at my silly jokes and made all my clothes (not easy with a tomboy daughter whose only requirement for anything wearable was: can I climb a tree in it?). Her love was a still point around which my life revolved.

Until everything changed.

I was twenty-seven and on a surf trip in Western Australia the day I found out Mum had cancer. It was early, a blue-sky morning. I was sitting on my surfboard waiting for my next wave, at a beach on the outskirts of Esperance, when I saw two men in khaki uniforms walking towards the water. *Strange*, I thought. They waved at me. *What's going on?* I caught a wave and rode it all the way to the beach. Bending down to unfasten my legrope, I noticed the men's shiny black shoes – police officers' shoes – sinking into the wet sand. When I straightened up, one of the men told me to call my father right away.

It was the early 1990s and it was a half-hour drive to the nearest payphone, in town. I worried the whole way. A few days earlier I'd received a letter from Mum, addressed to the caravan park where I'd been camping with my boyfriend, telling me she'd had a cough and needed to have some tests. It was 'all a bit scary,' she'd said. But why did I have to call *Dad*? That worried me the most.

I dialled the number I knew by heart. Mum's voice answered, newly croaky. The test results had come back. I heard the words 'malignant' and 'untreatable' and a fog enveloped us. We both cried. And I kept crying, on and off, for days, as my boyfriend and I drove to Perth so I could catch a flight back to Sydney to be with her.

It was a long, breathless downhill year for my darling mum. The end came just before dawn one November morning. Dad, Tim and I had tried to sleep in vinyl chairs beside her bed at the hospice all night, but it was when we reluctantly ducked out for a quick breakfast that she slipped away. We'd had time to prepare, but it still felt sudden and too soon for the person who had glued our family together, the one who had always been there, for all of us, to be gone.

We held her hands and smoothed her hair and hugged each other and cried. Then I drove to the beach alone. I hadn't surfed in weeks and the sea was wild that morning, but I had to be in the water. I wasn't OK. Nothing was OK. Paddling out, I felt awkward and bumped my nose against my board and it hurt and I wanted it to, wanted physical evidence of the pain inside, the emptiness inside. When I got out past the break, I sat staring at the horizon, feeling desperately alone. Then came the sobbing, as if from outside me at first. I listened to it, with the cold salty wind in my face and large unbroken waves breathing under me, as it drew closer and became louder and engulfed me and I became nothing while the sea, like a faithful friend, held me.

After the funeral, after all the visits and the phone calls and the days off work, life began to resume its normal dimensions. But I couldn't go back to 'normal'.

For months I was awash with grief – and an unexpected clarity. Although it had broken me, every day, to be with Mum in those final weeks as she'd spiralled like a falling leaf towards the end of her life, there'd been no doubt in my mind about where I needed to be, what I needed to do next, for her. Nothing had felt more real. A veil had been lifted; I could suddenly see everything more clearly and everything unimportant fell away, leaving only what mattered, and that made me feel alive.

I didn't know what any of this meant, only that I wanted to hold onto that sense of aliveness and clarity for as long as I could. And that I had to leave my job. My science degree, with a major in psychology, had led me into market research and although I liked the work, it didn't make sense to me anymore. So I quit and became someone who was twenty-eight years old with no idea what she wanted to do or what kind of life she wanted. She just knew it wasn't the one she'd been living.

Mum's death catapulted me into what I came to think of, years later, as my real life, by giving me a free pass to find out who I really was, to do something I'd never done before. And that first something was to live in Japan. I didn't speak a word of Japanese or have any Japanese friends or know anything about the country beyond the stereotypes. But I was young enough to apply for a working holiday visa. So I leaped into the unknown.

On the island of Kyushu, I rented a room on the outskirts of a small city called Miyazaki. It had a tatami-mat floor and a small kitchen, and I slept on a cotton futon I had to roll up every morning and stash in a cupboard so I'd have enough space to move around. Next door was a wetsuit factory, which is how I found my way into the small community of Japanese and *gaijin* (foreign) surfers in the area. We'd all surf together in the mornings and teach English in the afternoons and evenings. On summer Sundays, the subtropical air thick with humidity, we'd swim in the local river and have bento-box picnics under the trees. When the weather was cooler, we'd do weekend hikes in the volcanic hills, stopping on the way home to soak at a local *sento* (bathhouse) or to fill containers with water from a roadside stream.

Whenever I rode my bike to the nearest black-sand beach to check the surf, I'd stop to greet the *obaachans* I'd see on the way. Permanently stooped from planting rice their whole lives, these elderly women would peer up at me from under their wide-brimmed hats and act surprised to see a *gaijin* in their midst, despite seeing me almost every day. It was part of a little game we played.

'*Konnichiwa, Lou-chan!*' they'd say, crinkling their weathered faces.

We'd chat a little, they'd compliment my rudimentary Japanese and we'd all laugh at the ridiculousness of me being there. I must have looked completely alien to them – foreigners were even called 'resident aliens' back then – but I felt surprisingly at ease in Japan and accepted for being the kind of person I am, more than I ever had in Australia.

It was a simple, carefree, communal life. For the first time in a long time, I wasn't striving to get somewhere else. Happiness seemed to be right where I was, any day of the week, embedded in the simple act of doing exactly what I was doing.

When my working holiday visa expired, part of me felt ready to return to Australia after eighteen months away, but I'd never been so heartsick to leave a place. In losing Mum and one kind of home, I'd stumbled on another, one that was intertwined with the particulars of the time I was there, the people I was with. Still, Miyazaki stayed with me long after I left, my memories morphing into visions of recreating, somewhere else, the kind of life I'd had there – perhaps with a small wooden house by the sea, tatami-mat floors and paper walls, and a community of like-minded friends. For the first time, I started imagining a home for myself, unconsciously furnishing it with ideas of what I most valued and wanted to feel happy and safe. So began my quest to find it.

⌂

There was another element in this prelude to my tiny house story. When I returned to Sydney after Japan, I was determined not to return to market research or any other kind of 'proper' job, and because I'd written a few articles about Miyazaki for a foreigners' magazine in Japan, I decided to try travel writing.

I loved it, and not just for the places I was able to visit. I loved the work, learning about the world, crafting my stories, the sense of purpose it gave me. Travelling simplified my life, too. I always had a bag packed, ready to go; I never planned more than a month or two ahead. I chose freedom over security.

As the years rolled on, I felt more at home when I was away than when I was actually at home, which was usually a share house in Sydney, the only kind of housing I could afford on my freelance income. My father and brother lived nearby, but after Mum died we became fragments of a family that didn't really exist anymore; Dad remarried, Tim got married and started a family of his own, and I created a family out of my friends, people I could be myself with, people I could count on.

Then things started to shift under me. I started waking up in gorgeous hotel rooms in a panic, unable to remember where I was. I'd dissolve in a fit of crying in the shower before a breakfast meeting. I'd guiltily order room service instead of exploring a new city. I found myself thinking: *What am I doing here?* Closely followed by: *What's wrong with me?*

I was lucky, I told myself. I had work that I loved – a rare thing – and people who loved me, even if I never got to see them. But the truth kept bobbing to the surface: I was tired, lonely and burned out from the endless struggle to make ends meet.

So, in the middle of 2013, after two decades of living this life, I took a break. I was forty-eight, my beloved Burmese cat – one of the few constants in my world – had just died and my latest, longer-than-usual relationship, with a mountain guide had finally ended in tears and disappointment, on both sides (I had a habit of falling in love with tour guides whose lives were as nomadic as mine). If I'd needed an extra shove, it came when the house I'd been living in for ten years, with an ever-changing cast of housemates, was sold.

I gave away most of my belongings, stored the rest, handed the key to the estate agent and hit the road.

It might sound counterintuitive to keep travelling after having felt so unhappy on recent trips, but travel – and work – had long been my anchor. If I could just get back to first principles, I thought, reconnect with the kind of travel I'd done before I turned it into a job, I might discover where to go next in my life.

There was also this: all over the world I'd met expats in beautiful places and listened to their love stories. Because it was always love that had led them there. They'd fallen in love with the mountains or the people or a particular someone and they *just knew* they had to stay and make a life there. I kept waiting for that to happen to me. I'd loved a lot of places, a lot of people, had tried to stay open to possibilities. Part of me believed that if I just kept looking, I'd eventually find the place I was meant to be.

My first stop was Bali, simply because I'd won a flight there in a travel writing competition and I could afford to stay there for a while. Just outside Ubud, in the island's green centre, I moved into a sprawling guesthouse owned by an eccentric Chinese professor who lived in a book-lined attic apartment and claimed to have known Agatha Christie when they'd both lived in a hotel in Istanbul. One morning he invited me to join him for coffee in his dusty eyrie.

'You're on sabbatical!' he declared when I told him I was a travel writer taking a break from my regular life to, well, travel and write (I was still writing the occasional travel story from the road). I liked the sound of that, the Sabbath-like sense of rest and rejuvenation in it.

I stayed at the professor's guesthouse for a month and didn't write a single word. It felt liberating to be away and *not* looking for story angles or taking photos. Instead I took yoga classes and swam in the pool and hung out with new friends in 'wellness' cafes. I was doing what I never usually did: what most people do on their holidays. Except I didn't feel as if I were on holiday. I felt as if all the fun things I was doing were happening a short distance from where I was, with an invisible barrier between us, stopping me from actually feeling the fun in them.

So I kept moving, living off my meagre savings, and found myself increasingly attracted to small lodgings, and not just because of my small travel budget.

In Thailand I spent a few weeks in a cute cottage right on the beach and just big enough for a queen-sized bed under a pink mosquito net and a pair of French doors that opened onto a small deck. Then a friend in Switzerland invited me to house-sit for a month and instead of staying in his three-storey chateau, I moved into the sweet little guest chalet in the garden; it had antique skis and ice axes fixed to the walls, reindeer-motif bedspreads and big-mountain views from every one of its sweet little windows. I stayed in a tipi in Portugal, a train carriage in Sweden, a caravan in Croatia. But the more my surroundings changed, the less my travel-as-remedy plan seemed to be working.

On a brief visit to Sydney after nine months away, I bumped into a neighbour I hadn't seen in a while. He asked where I'd been lately. I rattled off a list of places.

'You seem a bit lost,' he said.

I bristled at his comment. He didn't know me at all, didn't know anything about my life. Travel writers travel, didn't he know that?

But he was right. I *was* lost.

For a year and a half I wandered. And in that sabbatical-of-sorts, something slowly, eventually, dawned on me. The more I moved around, the more I wanted to stay in each place, even when it didn't feel quite right. I was Goldilocks with too many options, restless in a way I'd never been before, searching for something solid under my wandering feet. That's when I found my little cabin in Norway and the first jigsaw piece of my personal puzzle fell into place.

Chapter 2

# The tiny house path

Back in Sydney after my sabbatical, after Norway and the cabin, I knew I couldn't stay; with housing becoming unreasonably expensive, I couldn't afford to live where I wanted to, I'd outgrown share houses, and I didn't want to go back to working too much just to cover the rent. So I left my home city again, packed up my car with my tent and a longboard I'd barely ridden in two years and headed up the coast on a surf trip. No itinerary, no plan. Just a quiet hope that camping and being solo in nature might put me on the right track again, maybe lead me to a place where I could bring my cabin dream to life. With any luck, I thought, I'd stumble upon a Miyazaki-like coastal village I could settle in for a while.

A few weeks later I drove past the CHEER UP, SLOW DOWN, CHILL OUT sign on the road into Byron Bay in northern NSW. I'd never planned to live on the north coast, but as soon as I got there I knew I had to stop moving. In an odd twist of fate, Mum had grown up in nearby Murwillumbah, in the foothills of Wollumbin (Mount Warning). Maybe she was calling me home one last time. That's how it is sometimes; we think life is linear, one thing happening after another, until something reminds us it's really a circle. But Murwillumbah was too far from the ocean for my salty soul, so I circled back to the coast and rented a studio apartment in a seaside village just south of Byron Bay.

It was the first time I'd lived in regional Australia and it surprised me how much I liked it. It was lush, uncrowded country, my new hometown flanked by dairy farms and pockets of coastal rainforest. There was a freshwater lake the colour of black tea at one end of the main street that ran alongside the beach, so close the sea breeze would regularly blow sand into the shops. I liked that you could leave your car unlocked when you walked, barefoot, into the small supermarket, where you'd invariably bump into someone you knew – and that people had time to chat. I liked that while doing everyday tasks like popping into the post office or the library, your gaze would invariably be drawn to the ocean. And I liked that living in a small town was much more affordable than living in a big city like Sydney.

I started travel writing again, but differently, wringing every last story idea from every trip to minimise the number of trips I did, and my carbon emissions, but also to limit my time away. I wanted to find the right balance between travelling to make a living and staying home to make a life.

A few months later, the housing crisis spilled out of the cities and started spreading across Australia, pooling in regional areas. The cost of living climbed. Rents increased. My landlady talked about selling the studio I was renting, which terrified me. Moving out would have meant leaving the community I'd started to feel part of. Life was beginning to feel precarious again.

Then I turned fifty. After successfully managing years of uncertainty in the holy trinity of steadying influences – my living situation, my love life and my work – I started to crave security.

Or maybe I just grew up. I'd always been a late bloomer, arriving late at all the major milestones in my life: first boyfriend, first kiss, first sexual encounter. Maybe this was just me, once again, taking my own sweet time to finally realise what other people my age had known for years: owning your own home really does matter, for reasons I didn't yet fully understand.

My curiosity started poking its nose into alleyways of alternative housing. With my Norwegian cabin in mind, I collected articles and bookmarked websites about people who had built small homes cheaply, out of recycled windows or old tyres filled with earth. I did a natural building course, thinking that I could build myself a little sustainable dwelling of some kind.

The problem was, I had no land, and no money to buy any.

Then, a blip on my radar: tiny houses built on trailers.

The more I learned about these 'tiny houses on wheels', the more they made sense to me. They were much less expensive than any other kind of house, for one thing, promising liberation from the rental hamster wheel without the financial burden of a mortgage. They were well designed, to make the most of a small living space. I loved their built-in sustainability ethos, too. Because they were on wheels, tiny houses didn't require any land clearing. Because they were small, they needed fewer building materials than regular houses, and less energy to heat and cool them after they were built. And they encouraged a minimalist mindset; less space meant living with less stuff, which in turn gave you more time to do whatever you wanted to do with your one wild, precious life.

I'd always tried to live as sustainably as I could, acutely aware of the impact of my travels on the planet. But I was becoming increasingly uncomfortable with flying. I had to face my own inconvenient truth: my working life just wasn't sustainable. Living in a tiny house seemed a way to rebalance the equation. If I could reduce my living costs, I thought, I could travel less, maybe even find work that didn't involve flying all over the world several times a year.

Also, we're hard-wired to live in small spaces. For most of human history, people have lived in small, simple structures made by hand, from materials close to hand. When we came down from the trees and out of the caves, we moved into huts made of sticks, mudbricks and animal hides; our homes were grass-clad domes, log shacks and stone houses designed to shelter us from the elements, from predators and from other humans. It's only recently that our dwellings have become mega-mansions (the average new house in Australia has a floor area of about 230 square metres, more than *ten times* the floor space of an average tiny house). To me, tiny houses weren't a backward step; they were a return to a way of living that could reconnect us with the natural world and remind us of our place in it.

I had no idea yet how it might happen, but for the first time in my life, owning my own home suddenly seemed within reach.

Chapter 3

# The start of us

Sometimes life has a way of sidling up to you and dropping something in your lap you hadn't been expecting. I'd been toggling back and forth between travelling and researching tiny houses, and settling in to my new community, when, six months after I'd moved north, I met Max.

It was a sunny Saturday morning and I was chatting with a few surfers I knew, in a car park by the beach, when an old white ute pulled up beside us. The first things I noticed about the driver as he greeted everyone, one elbow resting on the rim of his open window: a crooked nose still covered in zinc after his surf, a cheeky smile, eyes hiding behind dark glasses, a tattered straw hat. He seemed friendly and slightly aloof at the same time and even then I could tell he was unapologetically his own person.

'Lou, have you met Max?' someone said. 'Max, Lou.'

'Howdy, Lou,' said Max, stretching out one lean, muscled arm to shake my hand. I smiled and shook his hand. It was rough and weathered, a hand used to doing practical, outdoorsy things. I liked that.

I'd heard about Max before that day, and that he made hollow wooden surfboards, the kind the old-timers used to ride in the 1930s and 1940s. He could ride them too, apparently, which takes great skill. *Impressive*, I thought. I'd also heard that he had a partner, so when we finally met that Saturday morning, I filed Max in my mind under 'new friend'.

Before long, however, our daily routines began accidentally overlapping. This wasn't as obvious as it sounds; even in a small town, it was still possible to *not* see someone you knew for weeks at a stretch, so the fact that our lives kept bumping into each other had an air of serendipity about it. In the surf, we'd find ourselves sitting side by side on our boards on sparkling early mornings, waiting for waves. At the lake, we'd see each other after a late afternoon swim and end up leaning against our cars, under the paperbarks, talking until dusk. We could talk about anything. And our words kept finding common ground; neither of us had ever married or had children (unusual at our ages – I was fifty-two, he was fifty-six), we both loved books and reading, we liked to live simply, quietly, sustainably. I respected that he had a partner and neither of us would have crossed that line, but there was an undeniable electricity between us, a connection that buzzed like a live wire whenever we were near each other.

One afternoon, I mentioned to him that I liked singing and he invited me to a jam session at his house with a few guys I knew. Monday nights, a regular thing.

'We need backing vocals,' he said, reading my reluctance. I hadn't sung in front of anyone since choir practice at school, but something about his invitation, his wanting me there, made me agree.

As I walked up his driveway the following Monday, I felt a tingle of nervous excitement that would come to feel familiar over the next few years. I put it down to stage fright that night, but it turned out to be a fun, low-key evening, five of us playing and singing songs we all knew, with printed words on music stands and cords from electric guitars, amps and microphones snaking across the floor. I'd found another thing I liked doing with Max; we might have been just friends, but our voices curled around each other like lovers.

When I had to go away for work a couple of months later, Max offered to drive me to the airport. I didn't read anything into it; he was always doing good deeds for his friends. But on the way there, he told me his partner hadn't been happy about this particular good deed. Understandable, I thought; being friendly with someone of the opposite sex can destabilise any relationship. Max didn't see it that way.

'I just told her, "Lou's a friend and that's all there is to it",' he said.

*Ouch*, I thought, on her behalf. But I couldn't help feeling a surge of joy. *He stood up for me.*

A couple of years later, Max's relationship ended and our life together began – with a misunderstanding. We were still just friends, but we'd been hanging out more than usual, so when Max offered to pick me up at the airport after another work trip, it felt different to the last time.

'I'd love that,' I said. Being met off a flight by someone *not* holding a card bearing my name was a novel experience for me. I started to look forward to it even before I left.

My destination this time was Lord Howe Island, off the NSW mid-north coast, one of my favourite little islands in the world. I'd been there twice before so I had more free time than usual, time I spent imagining Max there with me. I was falling, and trying not to fall too far, too fast.

We hadn't had any contact that week – there was no mobile reception or internet access on the island – so on my way home, in transit at Sydney airport, I sent him a message to let him know my flight was on time and to check he could still pick me up. No reply. I waited, tried not to keep looking at my phone. Just before boarding, I called him. No answer. No voicemail. *Stay calm*, I told myself. *He was busy. People forget things.* But, waiting for take-off, seatbelt fastened, I panicked. I sent a message to my friend Cam, asking him to pick me up. 'No worries,' he replied.

Before turning off my phone, I messaged Max to let him know. No reply. My heart went quiet on that hour-long flight.

Cam dropped me home and I'd just started unpacking, feeling slightly, unexpectedly, heartbroken – *was this thing with Max over before it had even begun?* – when there was a knock at the door. And there he was, smiling, on my doorstep. My stomach did a little backflip and I smiled back, not sure which feeling to show – happiness at seeing him or disappointment at the missed airport reunion – but before I could decide, he pulled me close for a hello hug, the best 'welcome home' I'd had in a very long time.

'Thought you might not feel like cooking tonight,' he said, reaching into his bag and handing over a vegetarian curry he'd made for me. Thoughtful, kind. Two of the things I already loved about him. After untangling our crossed wires – he'd planned to pick me up as we'd agreed, hadn't checked his phone until he was about to leave for the airport, *hadn't forgotten me* – we stood in my kitchen, arms wrapped around each other for a second time that afternoon.

'How about a picnic dinner one night this week?' he said. Our first date.

'Tomorrow night?' I was keen to start whatever this was, or find out what it wasn't, as soon as possible.

The sun was just setting as we drove up to the headland in his ute, found a spot overlooking the sea and spread a rug on the grass. We sat close and unpacked our homemade picnic and ate and talked, and he said we probably shouldn't kiss because he'd only broken up with his ex a couple of months earlier, was still recovering from the breakup, but our faces drifted close, everything went out of focus and... it felt completely natural to kiss him, as if we'd been doing this all our lives. At the same time, alone in my bed that night, I felt changed in some way, like I was suddenly on a new path. And as I closed my eyes, one thought twirled around in my head and all through my body: I'd found my person.

Chapter 4

# The decision

Headlights on against the stormy gloom, Max and I drove through pelting rain, into the Southern Highlands just south of Sydney, following muddy roads that led, eventually, to an open farm gate. We parked his van (the ute had recently died) next to a barn before loading our overnight bags and a few supplies into a small wheeled cart. Then we set off on foot – me holding a large umbrella over our heads, Max pulling the cart – along a bush track that soon emerged at an impossibly green meadow.

And there in the middle of it, in a sudden shaft of light as the clouds miraculously parted, was a very small house called Edmond.

It was early 2019 and I'd been obsessing about tiny houses for a year. I'd completed a how-to-build-a-tiny workshop ('tiny' being a shorthand term for 'tiny house'). I'd watched countless tiny house tours, clips about interior design for small spaces, and documentaries about minimalism and simple living. But there was one thing I hadn't done. I'd never spent the night in a tiny.

To remedy this, and try out different kinds of tiny houses, Max and I decided to do a road trip south to Melbourne, our route determined by the locations of four tiny stays I'd booked: two in NSW, two in Victoria.

We'd been together for almost two years and although the good times had been more than good – they were everything I'd ever wanted in a relationship, everything we'd both wanted – we'd had more than our share of ups and downs, which made me feel nervous about going away with him, being alone with him, for a month. I wasn't sure we were ready for this.

'It'll be good for us,' he said, and eventually his optimism won me over. He wasn't blind to our troubles, but I think we both hoped that this trip would turn things around, that the constant togetherness would burn away our differences and leave us, at the end of it, with a clearer sense of who we were, and could be, together.

Plus, I was excited about the real purpose of the trip: to sweep away any lingering doubts about tiny house living and help me decide if this was something I really, truly wanted to do.

So, Edmond. A gingerbread-like tiny with a classic gable roof and huge picture windows, plonked in the kind of meadow that makes you want to lie on the grass all day making daisy chains and thinking unimportant thoughts. Despite being only 5.4 metres long, Edmond (tiny house weekenders often have names, I learned) was surprisingly spacious inside. I loved the high ceilings, those big windows, the green views from each one, the ladder up to its sleeping loft. There was a compact but perfectly functional kitchen, a rainwater-fed shower, solar panels on the roof and a composting toilet that smelled of nothing but sawdust.

The rain returned later that afternoon, giving us the perfect excuse to put the kettle on and cosy up on the L-shaped couch. We turned off our phones and read, cooked up some pasta for dinner and played Scrabble. It was a long night, in a good way.

After all I'd read and learned about tiny houses, nothing compared to the simple joy of staying in one, if only for a couple of nights. I liked climbing up to the sleeping loft and a proper queen-sized bed, listening to the rain pattering on the roof just above our heads, and opening the skylight first thing in the morning, after the storm had passed. Of course, part of the joy came from Edmond's pastoral location, but another part came from just being in a thoughtfully designed space.

I could see how tidy and organised you'd need to be if you lived in a house this small. Max and I developed a little floor-sharing dance, cross-stepping out of each other's way while we cooked and moved around in the tiny, which was fun. And that, ultimately, was the take-home message from our first tiny house stay: it was fun. When it was time to leave and we wheeled our little red wagon back across the impossibly green meadow to the van, I thought: *For all their clever design features and green credentials, there's something gloriously unserious about tiny houses.* And we still had three more to try.

When I was in my twenties, I had a boyfriend who delighted in saying, whenever we found ourselves in a small space of any kind – even, once, an elevator – 'I could live here'. It was a declaration of his independence from regular-sized homes and his desire to live an unconventional life, decades before tiny houses or other alternative dwellings became a thing. I don't know what kind of home he ended up living in, but his words became a guiding light for me while Max and I tiny-hopped our way south.

At each stop I asked myself: *Could I live here?*

The answer wasn't always yes, mainly because these tiny houses were built for weekends away, not for living. So there wasn't much storage space, one had a noisy exhaust fan on its composting toilet that kept me awake at night, and did I really want to climb a *ladder* to my bed every night for the rest of my life? One tiny was fossil-fuel-free, which was inspiring. Another had a fragrant cedar-panelled bathroom that smelled like a sauna. Every idea, whether I liked it or not, made me think about the features I might want in my own tiny.

Our last stop was just north of Melbourne, in a gully of gnarled eucalypts beside a drought-dry river. Modelled on wilderness huts sprinkled along hiking trails in Scandinavia, 'Micah' was basically a black wooden box with big windows, in a paddock, its wheels artfully concealed by rows of neatly stacked firewood. Inside, it was also disarmingly simple, but missing one classic tiny house feature. There was no loft. Instead, the queen bed occupied a waist-high platform at one end of the tiny. Accessible by a single step that doubled as a seat, it was flanked on two sides by bed-to-ceiling windows, which made it more than just a place to sleep.

After an early dinner by the campfire, relaxing in Adirondack chairs while sheep swarmed around us, Max and I snuggled up on the bed to watch the full moon rise from behind the nearest hill. The next morning we watched the sequel, a golden sunrise, without even lifting our heads from the pillows. I've always been wary of skylights, because of the potential for leakage in heavy rain, and Micah showed me that with your windows facing the right direction and your tiny positioned just so, you could still sky-watch from your bed, a lesson I would soon be applying when I started designing my own tiny home.

The road trip was a success in one way – it confirmed for me that I *did* really, truly want to live in a tiny house – but not in another.

From the moment we'd pulled away from the kerb at Max's place, something felt off between us. There was so much I loved about him. I loved that he felt things deeply and cried watching movies, and that he kept a dictionary by his bed, and had another in his van – and often looked up words just for fun, not just when he was reading. His affinity for the natural world meant I learned something new every time we were outdoors together, and I loved that he'd lived in the same modest house for fifteen years and had turned his front lawn into a permaculture garden to grow food. I teasingly called him my 'Renaissance man' because he was a seriously good surfer and rock climber, and an environmental scientist by profession (retired), who could write songs and play the guitar, use a sewing machine, give excellent massages (he'd once worked as a massage therapist) *and* make a timber cabinet in an afternoon.

But there were other things I was just starting to see. As we headed south along the freeway that day, he became suddenly stern with me, preoccupied with final practical details. The way he took charge seemed to suck the excitement out of our departure and made me feel as if this was his trip and I was just along for the ride.

I tried to tell myself everything would be OK, to accept the anxious itch under my skin, to remember that things would settle soon enough. But as the days and weeks rolled on, the times when we weren't connecting began to outnumber the times when we were.

When I told him I felt depressed, he was understanding and supportive, but there was a deeper truth I didn't want to face: being with *him* seemed to be making me depressed. There was something about the way we interacted. The way he spoke to me. It triggered old, familiar feelings I'd had growing up, but it was also just... us.

The turning point came just outside Melbourne. We were staying with one of Max's friends, a guy I hadn't met before, who took us sailing one afternoon in Port Phillip Bay. Just being on the water – flying across the sea, salt water spritzing my face, my hair wilded by the wind – made me feel like myself again. Back at the friend's house that evening, I booked a flight home.

Taking action eased my angst. The next day, before I caught a train to the airport, Max and I talked about the trip, the best talk we'd had in three weeks. I almost didn't want to leave, but amid the swirl of contradictory feelings, I was sure of two things: I loved him and I needed to not be around him, for a week or so at least.

At home, I found my footing again in my own life while Max dawdled back up the coast in his van. Now that he was alone, he was warmer towards me, sent me photos of his camping spots, wished I was there. I missed him, too. And by the time he got back, I was OK. We were OK.

⌂

One morning, a year later, I stepped out of bed and into a puddle. My tiny house plan had stalled after our road trip. Although I was still committed to it, real life kept getting in the way; I was writing as much as I could to save enough money to buy a tiny house trailer, but because I was still paying rent, that was taking longer than expected.

So life gave me a nudge to get me back on track.

It had been raining for days and although my studio had leaked before, I'd never seen it like this. Rubbing sleep from my eyes, still trying to wake up, I looked down at my feet. They really were wet. And so was everything else. I took a mental inventory: one floor rug, underwater; one large puddle creeping across the polished concrete floor towards a wooden bookcase; water wicking up the legs of a cane chair in the corner of my bedroom; more water trickling down one wall. Tiptoeing into the lounge room, trying not to slip on the wet floor, I looked up and saw black mould beginning to spread across the ceiling like a bruise.

As I started mopping up and moving furniture, listening to drips plinking into saucepans and buckets, I thought, with more urgency than ever before: *I've got to find somewhere else to live.*

A month later, in March 2020, the world stopped.

I was sitting at my desk, writing the last of my travel stories from what would end up being the last of my overseas trips for longer than any of us knew back then, when cities started going into lockdown. Borders closed, planes were grounded, publications I'd been writing for went into 'sleep mode'. A great silence descended.

And a window of opportunity opened. As someone whose livelihood was affected by border closures, I was entitled to a wage subsidy from the government. An idea began to take shape: maybe, before the window closed again, I could take six months off to design and build a tiny house.

Max and I had talked about building a tiny together, sometime, in theory. It was always going to be my home, not ours; we often slept at each other's places, but living together was an option we'd ruled out early. Partly because he already had a house and partly because it was an all-welcome home, with friends constantly coming and going, for a cuppa or to play music or to stay for a night or a week; for me, being a writer as well as an introvert, my home was my sanctuary, a space for quiet time and solitude.

But we hadn't discussed where to build it. Until one afternoon soon after the pandemic hit. Max and I were sitting in the sun on his verandah.

'You could build your tiny house here,' he said, reaching for his cup of tea. 'In the driveway; it's a nice shady spot. You could live in it there too, if you want, until you find somewhere more permanent.' As if it were no big deal.

But it was a big deal to me. And incredibly generous. And the perfect plan. Or it would have been if our relationship had been more stable. We'd never fully regained our balance after that road trip, although we were trying to, and on days like these, when the love was flowing strongly between us, I started to believe this just might work.

And if it didn't? Much as I wanted a tiny house, more than I've ever wanted anything, the possibility that this might *not* work made it appealing on another level.

I'd always been a moth to the flame of adventure, the kind defined as 'a risky undertaking of uncertain outcome'. I devoured books and films about polar, sailing and mountaineering expeditions that stripped life back to its essentials. Some of my favourite adventure stories didn't even involve much action, just a deep settling into one's surroundings by, say, living for a year in a bark hut in the Australian bush or spending six wintry months in a cabin by Lake Baikal in Siberia.

My work had often taken me to remote natural places – I'd sea kayaked in the Arctic and Papua New Guinea, trekked in Kamchatka and all over Nepal, paddled a canoe in Madagascar – but always with experienced guides. In my more daring moments, I imagined having an unsupervised adventure of some kind, cracking myself open on the edge of a big challenging experience and finding inside the unconditioned me I longed to be all the time. Sometimes, usually when I was in transit, idling in the no-man's-land between leaving one place and not yet arriving in another, I'd wonder: *What could my adventure be? A long walk, a long voyage, a long time in a wild place?* I wanted to let it find me, without forcing it to come, but I always assumed it would be something I'd do alone, in a faraway place.

Until the pandemic, and Max's offer, sent my thoughts in a new direction.

*Maybe building a tiny house is the adventure I've been waiting for*, I thought. It seemed a risky enough proposition to qualify. I didn't yet have enough money to fund the build, or land to eventually move the tiny to. I had no building skills. I was diving deeper into a relationship that had already proved rickety and might not be able to bear the ongoing stress of building a house. Besides, distant lands were, in some ways, familiar to me. Being at home, staying in one place, that had always been more of a challenge.

I had two more things in my favour. Time, and plenty of it now that the pandemic had cancelled life as we knew it. And someone who loved me enough to do this difficult thing with me.

I studied Max's face for signs that he was serious. He smiled.

'Thank you!' I smiled back. This felt right, and good. 'Let's do this.'

# PART 2
# BEGINNING

*'All journeys have secret destinations of which the traveller is unaware.'*
~ Martin Buber

Chapter 5

# A hand-drawn plan

As the world settled into lockdown, I settled into the process of designing my little home. It felt like a full-time job and in the absence of any travel writing work I treated it as one, just for the get-out-of-bed sense of purpose it gave me. Before long I realised there was nothing else I'd rather be doing, nowhere else I wanted to be.

One of the things that first attracted me to tiny houses was that you could, theoretically, build one yourself, with your own hands and a few power tools.

That had practical advantages. With both Max and I working on the tiny full-time – he wasn't a builder but was always making things and had all the tools we'd need – and occasional help from a few tradie mates, I figured we could do the build for as little as sixty or seventy thousand dollars. Plus a few months of our lives. For the true cost of a thing, as Henry David Thoreau famously said, is 'the amount of what I will call life which is required to be exchanged for it, immediately or in the long run.' When I thought about it like that, building the tiny ourselves sounded like an unbelievably good deal.

It would also allow us to tweak the design and fix our mistakes as we went along; if a feature wasn't working or didn't look as good in three dimensions as it had on paper, we could change it.

Best of all, the build would be an experience. Fred Schultz, who pioneered the tiny house movement in Australia in 2015, talked about this in his tiny-building workshop, the one I did in 2019. 'The tiny house movement is about reclaiming shelter-making,' he'd said. 'It's about making use of this little crack in the regulations that allows us to build our own homes and putting the hammer back in the hands of people to reclaim this part of our lives.'

That little crack in the regulations also meant I could draw my own plans; because tiny houses on wheels are classified as vehicles not buildings, the national building code doesn't apply to them and there's no need to submit build-ready plans to anyone for approval. (I did, however, use Fred's tiny-house-on-wheels building method and followed the national design rules for caravans, called the Vehicle Standards Bulletin 1.)

Of course, I could have used design software or bought a tiny house plan online, but designing my home was, for me, an integral part of this whole adventure. So in late March, I made my first purchase for the build – a pad of graph paper – and began, tentatively, drawing.

The more I drew and measured and erased and redrew my plans, the more I learned about my tiny house. A few months later, as we approached the build's start line, I'd lift my gaze off the floor plan and draw the tiny from other angles to make sure all my windows lined up, check the slope of my roof or help me visualise the interior fit-out. But for now my focus was on what was essentially a rectangle on a page and how I was going to fit my entire life inside it.

There's a magnificent sense of possibility when you set out to design and build your own home, no matter how big or small it is. (I settled on a fairly standard 7.2-metre tiny: big enough to be comfortable, small enough to be easily moved.) *For the first time in my life*, I thought, *I'll be able to have exactly the kind of home I've always wanted.* But what kind of home *did* I really want and what did I truly need?

Years ago, I travelled with a journalist who liked to completely unpack his suitcase wherever he stayed, even if it was just for a night. He'd decant every possession he'd brought with him into the room he would probably spend only a few hours in, most of them sleeping. He'd put his clothes in the drawers and the closet, a book he was reading on the bedside table, his toiletries in the bathroom. It made him feel at home, he said. It seemed like a lot of trouble to go to, I thought, and made speedy exits tricky if you, say, slept through your alarm and had a plane to catch.

But I liked the sentiment. And he was right, in a big-picture sense: for that one night, a fragment of his life, that hotel room *was* his home. That's how I came to see the spaces I temporarily inhabited on my travels in the year or so before the pandemic hit. I'd lie in bed wherever I was – a micro-hotel in Tokyo, perhaps, or a shipping container hostel in Bangkok – and take in the room's layout, the size of its windows, the shape of the light fittings. *What did I really need beyond a bed, a bathroom, a desk and a window that opened?*

Instead of buying souvenirs, I'd bring home design ideas from the places I stayed. Tatami mats from Japan, louvre windows from Darwin, furnished terraces from India.

Trekking in Mongolia once, I came upon a family of nomads preparing to relocate to greener pastures, for their livestock. Due for a rest stop, my companions and I shrugged off our packs and watched the nomads dismantle their home. (We didn't offer to help; they didn't need a bunch of clueless foreigners getting in the way.) First, they removed the felted walls of their ger, a traditional Mongolian tent. Then its skeletal frame was folded up and carefully stacked, leaving the family's beds and saucepans and clothes and radios and toys where they stood, on a neat circle of overlapping rugs no longer surrounded by walls, an island of human things in a grassy sea, ready to be loaded onto a truck for the short move. That image has lingered in my mind for more than ten years now, reminding me, like a visual mantra, of how little we really need.

Of course, all the design ideas in the world won't save you if you haven't done one essential, unavoidable thing: examine your own life and lifestyle. So I began thinking deeply, and widely, about how I currently lived, how I wanted to live and what was important to me. Starting with how I was living in my studio.

*Where did I spend most of my (non-sleeping) time when I was at home?* That was easy: at my desk and on the couch (the latter being my dining area as well as my lounging space). *How did I use my kitchen?* I made dinner more than I ate out and I loved being able to see bulk food items like rice and oats in glass jars on shelves within easy reach. *What did I like about my apartment?* Its sense of privacy and peace, the big desk under a big window, the sliding glass doors that opened onto a leafy garden, and the fact that I couldn't hear the fridge humming from my bed. *How much stuff did I need to store?* The big items were a couple of surfboards, some camping gear and a few plastic tubs of books. *How often did I have visitors, and what did we do together when they came over?* I mostly socialised outside my home, but I realised that I'd like to have the kind of place I could invite friends to, for conversational cups of tea and casual dinners.

Beyond my own four walls, I looked at my human-made surroundings in a whole new light. I took long walks just to look at other people's houses through the lens of whatever design feature I happened to be thinking about that week, whether it was windows or cladding or eaves. There was a new housing estate up the road and every house – or apartment block or shop – became a display home to me, from the outside at least. I managed to resist actually knocking on any doors asking to see inside, though there was an awkward moment at a local cafe when the (attractive, male) barista seemed to think I was staring at him when I was actually admiring the timber-framed gas-strut window through which he was handing customers their almond-milk lattes.

I loved this phase of the project. Saturday nights on the couch with Max watching online tiny house tours and learning about the architecture of small spaces. Early morning conversations in bed, waking up with solutions to design problems we'd had the previous day. At random moments, while having lunch or zipping up each other's wetsuits before a surf, one of us would say, 'What do you think about having a window above the sink?' or 'How about putting the couch on the *east* side of the house?' and we'd lose ourselves in tiny thoughts for a few long minutes before returning to what we'd been doing. We didn't always agree, but we were having fun sifting through the options.

Mostly I loved that Max and I were working on this together, collaborating and sharing ideas with each other. When we'd first started dating, we'd often surf and go snorkelling together, sing together, skinny dip at secluded beaches, do long side-by-side swims in the lake – before retreating to his place or mine, where we'd find a shady spot and curl up together for a nap. But in the months – *had it been longer?* – before we'd started designing the tiny, our clashes had become more frequent and we hadn't played together much.

I whispered to myself that creating something together might heal the cracks in our relationship. I know how this sounds: like having a baby when your relationship isn't ready, hoping an unsuspecting little being will uncork the love you both have inside. But we weren't trying to wallpaper over our problems or pretend they weren't there. We both wanted this tiny; Max really wanted me to finally have my own home and had told me he was looking forward to us building it together. And in my hopeful mind's eye, I saw this project as a way to take the focus off our issues and return us to a simpler way of being with each other, one in which we could enjoy doing things together, the way we had before.

Just as I was beginning to feel over-inspired by all the gorgeously styled tiny houses we kept seeing on YouTube – so many designs, so many space-saving features, so many possibilities! – I did a short online design course led by American tiny house architect Macy Miller. She suggested making a wishlist of features I *had* to have in my tiny, to help narrow the field of options. So I took a notebook, a pen and a chair into the spring sunshine at my place one afternoon.

The first item on my wishlist: plenty of natural light. I'd lived in too many dark, south-facing houses that were cool in summer, ice-cold in winter and gloomy all year round. Good air flow was vital for keeping the tiny as cool as possible during the long, rainy summers in northern NSW. Because I work from home, I wanted a dedicated workspace – not one that also served as a dining table or a kitchen bench – so I wouldn't have to tidy it up or fold it away every night. I'd need a comfy couch that was long enough to serve as a spare bed for overnight guests or if I was ever temporarily unable to climb the stairs to my loft. I'm a basic cook, but I love baking so I wanted lots of bench space; I figured I'd only need a two-burner stove, but I definitely wanted a full-size oven.

I've never in my adult life had a dining table, but I'd always wanted a kitchen table big enough to read a newspaper, work on a sewing project or have a friend or two over for dinner. In tiny terms, this meant having a long wooden bench that could do double-duty as my kitchen counter and dining area. Thinking ahead, I figured having stairs to my bed loft (a bed loft being another must) would be kinder to my body than a ladder, as I got older; they also offered more storage. And finally, open floor space downstairs, for stretching and doing yoga, as well as a 'lounge loft' where I could sit on the floor as I had when I'd lived in Japan. (Macy had said that, in addition to high ceilings, having some floor space free of built-ins can make a tiny feel more spacious.)

There was one more question my wishlist needed to answer: How did I want to *feel* living in my tiny? A home is more than the sum of its practical parts, after all.

I went back to my thinking place in the sun and came up with this: I wanted to feel safe and 'at home'. I wanted to feel connected to the natural world, to be aware, while I was inside, of what was going on outside; to see trees and sky through my windows, to hear the birds in the trees and the rain on the roof, to know which way the wind was blowing. I wanted the warmth of wood all around me and a cosy feeling when I climbed up to my bed loft every night. I wanted my tiny to be a place I could retreat to, and turn inward when I needed to. And I wanted it to be beautiful, if only to me, so that I'd feel happy whenever I stepped inside. All within 25 square metres, including the two lofts. So, you know, no pressure.

To round out my design brief, I made an *un*-wishlist of things I *didn't* want, so I could discard features I'd liked in other tiny houses but didn't need in mine.

To keep my energy usage low, I didn't want air-conditioning or an overhead fan; if I got my window configuration right, I figured I wouldn't need either. For the same reason I didn't need a dishwasher; I'd read about dishwashers saving water, but I'm always looking for ways to use less power. Besides, I like the nightly ritual of hand-washing the dishes and living alone means I never have too many to wash.

I could do without soft-close drawers, because I like the way mindfully closing a drawer, and other small actions, can help us pay attention to the everyday details of our lives. I've never owned a washing machine or a dryer, and I was perfectly content using a laundromat and letting my clothes line-dry in the sun (another way to stay connected to the natural world), so these also went onto my un-wishlist. Finally, I didn't want a gable roof; they look sweet, but I wanted the highest point on my ceiling to be on one side, above my stairs, not in the middle of the house.

At the end of all this thinking and winnowing of ideas, I could almost see my tiny, like a mirage in my mind. It would be a contemporary cabin with a gently sloping roof, as many windows as possible and an all-white interior offset by plenty of timber features. I imagined a large desk under a north-facing window, stairs leading to a sleeping loft, a lounge loft accessible by a ladder, and a galley kitchen. Outside, there'd be a deck with an outdoor shower, in addition to my indoor one. And I'd use sustainable/renewable materials wherever I could and go off-grid as soon as possible, starting with a compost toilet, and gas for cooking and hot water (stage two would involve solar panels and a rainwater tank, when finances allowed).

Now I just had to draw it.

Chapter 6

# Dream-killers

For all my simple-living intentions, designing my tiny ended up being way more complicated than I'd expected. It was more like designing a boat than a house, in terms of making the most of every bit of available space. There was so much to learn, research and think about. There were tiny-specific constraints, too, like how much my home could weigh when finished (it had to be less than 4.5 tonnes), where the front door could go (on the 'passenger' side, because tiny houses are classified as caravans) and where the heaviest features could be (such as the stairs and the kitchen cabinets) so the tiny would be safe to tow.

But constraints can be a good thing, I learned. Like lane markers or guard rails, they keep you on track and moving forward instead of fanning out in too many directions. There's liberation in limitation.

It took me a month of diligent thinking and a house call from a very patient sales rep, who happened to love tiny houses, just to decide on my windows. How many I wanted (thirteen), what the frames should be made of (aluminium, for low maintenance), the dimensions of each (varied), what type they should be (mostly awnings, so they could stay open when it was raining, an important consideration in the subtropics where most of the rain falls in summer) and, most importantly, where they'd go – because this would determine the location of other features in my tiny.

One thing you usually *don't* have to do when designing a regular house is decide, before you even move in, where all your furniture is going to go – and stay. But most of my furniture was going to be built-in: my couch, my desk, my kitchen table/bench. (The upside of this was that I'd never have to buy furniture again.) Similarly, having limited space means you need to consider little things you wouldn't bother thinking about before a normal build, such as where will you put your keys when you walk in the front door, where will you get dressed every morning and (this one I almost forgot) where will your laundry basket go?

Even when I'd decided roughly where to put all the main elements on my floor plan – the kitchen, the bathroom, the desk, the couch – I'd merely graduated to the next level of difficulty in this design game. To decide where the front door would go, for instance, I had to know where my kitchen cabinets would end, which required me to find out the standard dimensions of kitchen cabinets, take stock of all my kitchen appliances and food jars *and* figure out exactly how much bench space I might need.

But eventually, decision by decision, it all started coming together.

A couple of months into the design process, I showed my latest floor plan to one of Max's best friends. A nuggety Californian in his late sixties with soda-bottle glasses, a mop of sandy hair and a quiet manner, George had been a licensed builder for more than forty years and had offered to help us with the first part of the build, to make sure my tiny was structurally sound. He also has a creative heart and a good eye for aesthetics, so I wanted his advice before I progressed too far with my design.

When I handed him my floor plan, he held it in his gnarled builder's hands, squinted at my pencil lines for several long minutes and gently but firmly told me that a couple of the features I'd drawn weren't going to work. The position of some of the windows, for one thing, meant there wouldn't be enough uninterrupted wall space for all the sheets of bracing ply we'd need to put up to stabilise the external walls.

'Don't worry,' he said, in his raspy SoCal drawl, registering the disappointment on my face, 'I'm used to being the dream-killer'. He regularly had to tell clients they couldn't have everything they wanted, he said, usually for structural reasons.

I went back to my drawing pad.

Max wasn't a dream-killer like George, but I found it harder to accept when he didn't like my ideas. One morning, after staying up late finalising the position of all those windows, feeling pleased to have made progress on a tricky part of the design, I showed him my updated drawings. With the best of intentions, he told me everything that was wrong with them, said some of my ideas were ridiculous.

Inside, I felt the fizz of anxiety. Something was happening. Something familiar. *Calm down*, I told myself. *He didn't mean to hurt me. He cares enough to be honest with me. We're in this together.*

It wasn't just what Max had said about my plans, it was the way he'd said it, a tone in his voice, an attitude standing, arms-crossed, behind his words which seemed to come from above me and made me feel smaller than I'd felt a moment before. I knew that tone. 'You're imagining things', Dad used to say. 'Don't be so sensitive'.

One of the things I'd loved most about Max, right from the start, was that he was sensitive, too, and noticed slight shifts in my mood; he could tell when I felt even slightly bothered about something and he'd encourage me to share how I felt. 'Talk to me, Loui,' he'd say. And when I did, the way I saw the world became real again. But that dismissive tone could catch me off-guard and I was starting to hear it more often in Max's voice.

I didn't defend my plans that day, just sat on the couch beside him like a scrunched-up piece of paper. I was afraid to tell him how I felt. Worried that the conversation would escalate into an argument, as it increasingly did. Instead I just stood under the waterfall of my own unwanted thoughts, feeling overwhelmed. *What was wrong with me? Why was this so hard?*

Back at my place, just a few minutes' drive from Max's house, I spent the rest of the day redrawing my plans. He sent me a message late that night: 'You're doing a good job, Loui. This is difficult stuff, and all-consuming. Meltdowns are to be expected sometimes so don't be too hard on yourself and I'll try to hug you more.' I hadn't had a meltdown, but I tried to take in the care in his words and let the dark clouds pass.

Finally, after four months of drawing, thinking, researching and more drawing, Max and I marked out the floor plan, to scale, on the hardwood floor of his house to get a visceral sense for how everything fit together.

While he read out measurements, I used masking tape to outline all the features on the floor. Then I stepped through the 'front door' and walked past the 'kitchen', imagining the bench and the walls growing up around me from the taped lines at my feet. Max lay on the 'couch' to check it was long enough for him. I pretended to walk up the 'stairs' to my sleeping loft and washed a few dishes in the 'sink' to see if I had enough elbow room. And in this wall-less tiny house of mine, the walls between us came down; we were on the same team again.

A couple of weeks later, when the floor plan had changed again, I was walking along the beach and decided to mark it out on the sand, with a stick, on a whim. I knew it so well, I didn't need my drawings anymore. This design was in me. And now it was in nature, too, until the next high tide. As I walked around inside my little sand floor plan, a few seagulls joined me, wandering in and out through the 'walls' conducting their own inspection.

Late one Monday night soon after that, something clicked. I was sitting on my couch at home, tinkering with the floor plan yet again, but this time, when I put down my pencil and blew away the bits of eraser from all my rubbings-out, I looked at the design on the page and it felt… right. Houston, we had a floor plan.

Chapter 7

# One little thing at a time

*What the fuck am I doing? What made me think I could do this? I should be feeling confident before tackling a big project, before embarking on a big adventure, not... like this. I'm worried I'm not in the right frame of mind, worried about the relationship. I've been falling into depressive holes too often, watching anxiety do its jittery dance around my head too many times. What will happen when I add 'building a tiny house' to all this?*

I'd just ordered a purpose-built tiny house trailer: 7.2 metres, tri-axle, galvanised steel. My first big expense, it cost more than my car. To pay for it, I'd withdrawn some money from my super fund, thanks to new government rules introduced during the pandemic. There was no going back now. I wasn't standing on the edge of an unknown anymore. I was free-falling, tumbling down a rabbit hole of building terms and materials and tools and construction techniques.

And in the middle of an ordinary night, after an ordinary day of pre-build research, I panicked. *Who was I to think I could build a house, even a tiny one?* I switched on the light, found a pen and a scrap of paper, and started writing down all the prickly fear and the marshmallow uncertainty – it worked sometimes, helped to calm the choppy thoughts – and I kept writing, hoping self-soothing words would come and maybe a knowing about what to do next. And they did, sort of, just before I fell asleep again. When I woke up the next morning I read the last lines I'd written the night before. *A big thing is just a series of little things. Just take it one little thing at a time.*

While we waited for the trailer to arrive, I made a promise to myself: every day, I would do something to move me in the direction of my tiny, even if it was just watching another tiny house tour online or researching shower heads. *One little thing at a time.*

I was back in my comfort zone. My laptop was bursting at the seams with interior design ideas for small spaces. I borrowed books about architecture from the library. I did Fred's tiny-building course again, online this time, to consolidate everything I'd learned in the face-to-face workshop. I visited people in my area who lived in tiny houses, and asked them about their tiny-build experiences. Before I fell asleep each night, I read kitchen catalogues instead of novels, and when a sample of western red cedar, one of my cladding options, arrived in the mail I kept it beside my bed for a week, hoping its sweet, woody scent would infiltrate my dreams.

One morning I made my first official trip to the local hardware store to kit myself out with a toolbelt, safety glasses, earmuffs and a tape measure I started carrying around to measure couches, windows and tables I liked in shops, restaurants and friends' houses.

It was all intensely interesting. Who knew bench tops and doors and floorboards have standard dimensions? Or that builders talk in millimetres, not centimetres? After being a word nerd all my adult life, I loved learning the language of this new world and hearing myself say things like '600 centres' and 'timber profiles' and 'R-values' to building suppliers felt every bit as empowering as learning how to order a meal or buy a train ticket in a foreign country.

I'd been warned that the building industry was blokey, particularly in Australia, and braced myself for snide or sexist remarks and attitudes. They never came. Not even when I started asking questions no real tradie would ever ask (like: what does '600 centres' actually mean? Answer: when it's referring to your wall studs, those vertical timber posts in your house frame, it means they're 600 millimetres apart, measured from the centre of each one). Everyone I encountered during the build was helpful, friendly and respectful. And the more phone calls and visits to suppliers I made, the more confident I became at speaking 'builder'.

Day by day, week by week, all these little things added up. I was getting a clearer picture of exactly what my tiny would look like, what materials it would be made of, where I could order them. There were still dozens of decisions to make before we started building, but it was happening. More puzzle pieces were falling into place.

A couple of months before the start of the build, I was at the beach early one morning, just about to have a swim, when I bumped into a guy I knew. Nick and I weren't really friends, but we'd had a few thoughtful chats over the years and I liked him. He asked me what I was doing with myself now that I couldn't travel. I told him I was building a tiny house, still not used to saying it out loud.

'Actually, I'm just doing all the research and planning at the moment,' I said.

He nodded, then frowned. 'I know someone who built a tiny. Total disaster.'

As a landscaper, Nick knew a bit about construction and proceeded to tell me a cautionary tale of *two* builders who failed to finish his friend's tiny house, leaving her to repair their blunders herself and move in before the electricity and water were even connected.

'Sounds awful,' I said.

Then he started firing questions at me. Was I building my tiny on a trailer? Would the trailer be rust-proof? And roadworthy? Where was I going to park it? Where would my greywater go? What kind of toilet would I have? Would my house have a steel or timber frame? Was I going off-grid? And, my all-time favourite: why not just buy a caravan? (It's a fair question. Caravans tend to cost less than tiny houses and to many people a tiny is just an over-engineered caravan anyway. But I'd learned that tiny houses have some big advantages over caravans for anyone planning to live in one: they're built to shed water, like a regular house; they can have larger windows and more of them, even sliding doors and skylights; and their high ceilings enable them to have lofts, creating more living space on a small footprint.)

He was like one of those tennis machines that shoots fluffy yellow balls at you at a rapid rate, and I got the feeling he was trying to catch me out. But as his questions kept coming, I kept answering them, much to my own delight.

'Thanks, Nick,' I said, when he finally ran out of things to ask.

'What for?'

'For showing me how much I've learned. I wouldn't have been able to answer even half these questions two months ago.'

After we said goodbye, I walked onto the beach and stood for a minute at the water's edge before wading in. I was finally ready. Not ready to start building, not quite, but ready in my mind for this strange new project I'd committed myself to.

Chapter 8

# Women's (wood)work

Before this build, I'd never made anything out of wood. I'd never done a woodworking class. Or held a power tool of any kind. All of which, with the blind ignorance of a true beginner, made the experience ahead even more exciting to me. I knew I'd need a lot of help, but I also knew I wanted to be hands-on every step of the way, not watching from the sidelines while someone else built my tiny for me.

About a month before we were due to start building, Max and I were driving through town after a surf when he saw a guy he knew, Rob, walking his dog. Max pulled over and introduced us. The dog sat quietly on the footpath, panting.

'What've you been up to, mate?' Rob asked.

'George and I are about to build a tiny house,' Max replied. I was sitting right next to him and I wasn't there. The conversation fell off a cliff and I fell with it, down and away from where Max and this guy I didn't know were still talking.

Somewhere in the distance, I heard goodbyes. I probably smiled, automatic. We started driving away.

'Everything OK?' Max asked, noticing I was quiet.

'Why did you say you and George are building the tiny?' I tried to stop my voice from shaking.

He didn't answer, didn't look at me. I could sense trouble coming. *Slow down, slow down.*

'I don't understand. That's not what we've been talking about,' I said. *Try to keep calm.* '*We're* building it, you and me. With George's help when we need it, but it's our project. Right?'

'Well, George and I will be doing most of it,' he said, not apologising.

I felt it then, the sadness that had been under that first flash of anger. I didn't want it to be like this. I didn't know what else to say.

It was a short, silent drive back to his house. I'd already decided to get some skills under my new toolbelt so I wouldn't be a wallflower at the build, but this sudden threat – that I could be left out, left behind, on my big adventure – brought a new sense of urgency. That afternoon I booked myself into a woodworking workshop to be held the following Saturday.

'Hello, everyone,' said Sophie, our woodworking instructor for the day. Despite having more than a decade of experience in carpentry, building and architecture, she didn't look or act like any builder I'd ever met. She spoke softly with a posh English accent and wore a floral cotton shirt with her sturdy work pants and boots, and a handmade leather toolbelt around her hips. Her short curly hair looked ready to escape the confines of her pretty headscarf at any moment.

I'd signed up for a beginners' workshop at Shedding, a community project Sophie had set up in a semi-rural town not far from where I lived. It's basically a shed where people learn to 'shed' their inhibitions about making and although these workshops weren't just for women, all the participants that Saturday morning were female. Some wore overalls, some were just in jeans like me, but all of us had our hair safely tied back, as instructed.

'The first thing I want to say today is very important,' Sophie said, pausing for effect. 'Feelings are welcome. Tools are easy; it's emotions that can sometimes hold us back. So, how are you all feeling?'

One by one we mumbled about being 'pretty nervous' and 'excited' and 'worried I'll do something silly'. I felt a bit anxious, but mostly excited about what we were about to learn. Sophie listened to us all before introducing Shedding's 'positive mental health facilitator' – her placid black kelpie, Hoogs, who had just settled at her feet.

Then she asked us why we were doing the workshop.

Some of the women wanted to make furniture, some had gone through a breakup and wanted to be able to do the things their partners had always done around the house, one couple wanted to learn a new skill together. I felt oddly self-conscious telling the group I was about to build a tiny. It was an audacious goal for someone in a beginners' woodworking class. Also, tiny houses were fast becoming a thing; I didn't want my classmates to think I was just another dreamer riding the tiny house trend. But Sophie loved my goal; she lived in a self-built gypsy wagon herself.

'Before we start, let's get a few formalities out of the way,' she said. 'By doing this workshop, you're agreeing to three things: we celebrate mistakes, because that's how we learn; there are no assumptions and there's no shame (ask as many questions as you like); and, very important, *own* the tool in your hand. Whenever someone takes a tool out of your hand to show you how to do something, you don't learn and you might even feel stupid or angry with that person. That's *not* what we do here. We'll show you how to do things, but the tool in your hand is yours while you're holding it. Clear?'

We all nodded. I don't think I was the only one slightly girl-crushing on Sophie at this point.

Standing at the workbenches on the shed's sunny, open-sided verandah, we watched Sophie demonstrate a few basic skills before practising them ourselves on some scraps of wood. We learned how to mark up a plank using flat builder's pencils (they're flat to stop them rolling) and 'squares' (which are actually triangles used to ensure your cuts are perpendicular to the edge of whatever you're cutting). We cut a piece of wood in half with a hand-saw whose teeth pointed forward so it cuts when you *push*, then cut it in half again with a different saw that cuts on the *pull*, while Sophie told us that good sawing technique is like good sex: don't rush, feel your way, find a rhythm, build up speed... We all giggled and looked sideways at each other as we pushed and pulled our saws. Who knew woodworking could be such fun?

Finally we screwed our cut bits of wood together using power drills and impact drivers. This is how much of a complete and utter novice I was: before Sophie's workshop I hadn't known you can use drills to drill holes *and* insert screws; impact drivers are also multi-functional, I learned, but mostly used for *driving* screws into difficult places. I'd never even *held* a drill or an impact driver before. We learned how to choose the right-sized drill bits, how to drill 'pilot' holes and the all-important 'righty tighty, lefty loosey' rule. (Which is: to tighten a screw, turn it to the right; to loosen it, turn it to the left.) Drills and impact drivers even have reverse gears to remove screws. How could I have lived half my life without knowing all this?

'There's no "stoopid" here,' Sophie said with a Gomer Pyle accent as she strolled past our benches, checking on our progress. 'There's only "don't know yet".'

It wasn't all task-oriented learning. She encouraged us to be aware of our bodies as well as our feelings: to adjust the height of our workbenches if we needed to, to position our feet so we felt balanced before using a tool and to change our posture to stay comfortable as we worked our way along a length of timber. When I was having trouble with my impact driver – it kept bouncing off the head of the screw I was trying to insert – Sophie showed me how she sometimes presses her shoulder against the hilt of the driver and leans her body weight onto it, to keep it steady.

'It's perfectly fine to stop what you're doing if you don't feel quite right, for whatever reason, wriggle your shoulders around and start again,' she said.

We didn't actually make anything, but I left Shedding that afternoon with two things that were even more useful: new skills and a new way of looking at woodworking.

Just listening to Sophie, seeing her in action and working alongside other women normalised the whole 'women in building' thing for me. I'd known that women builders existed, but I'd only ever seen men using power tools and working on building sites, which made me believe I had to be like them – and made me worry I wouldn't be strong enough to use the big, heavy tools I'd be using on my build (which, admittedly, *are* mostly designed for men's hands and grip strength). Sophie changed all that, made it seem perfectly reasonable that anyone, with the right tools, a bit of knowledge and a willingness to learn and make mistakes, could make something out of wood or build their own furniture – or a tiny house.

On my way home, I vowed to remember that and use her holistic approach wherever I could in my build. And in the months ahead she became something of a build-angel to me whenever I felt unsure about what I was doing, which was almost every day. I'd stop, breathe, wriggle my shoulders and ask myself, 'What would Sophie do?'

Chapter 9

# First, build a chair

It was a wintry Monday morning. Max and I were in his garage preparing to upcycle two outdoor chairs, a pre-build project I'd wanted to do, to practise some of the skills I'd learned from Sophie and learn a few more from him. The plan was for us to take one chair each and replace the black plastic webbing on them with hardwood slats.

I was just starting on my chair, cutting away the webbing with a Stanley knife, when Max came over and took the knife out of my hand. He said he wanted to show me how to hold it properly, was worried I was going to hurt myself. I remembered what Sophie had said about teaching someone this way and she was right. I already had first-day nerves, and when Max took the knife from me I felt like a scolded child. Cue our first on-the-job conflict. I tried to explain why I didn't want him to take the knife; he counter-explained why he needed to. Things were starting to escalate. I could feel my heart beating.

'Just let me figure it out, OK?' I said, trying to sound more confident than I felt. 'Don't worry, I'm not going to cut myself.'

He wasn't fooled. 'You're acting like a ten-year-old,' he said, over his shoulder, already walking back to his house. 'I'm not going to work with you if you're like this.'

I took a few breaths, waited for my heartbeat to slow, then followed him up the short path to his house. Standing at the open door, not feeling welcome enough to step inside, I sent my words across the living room to where he was acting busy in the kitchen.

'What's going on? Are you OK?' I wanted to repair this rupture between us and get back to work. We could do this. I was already feeling calmer than I'd felt in the garage. But he didn't want to talk. Or reconnect. He was 'fine', he said – and done for the day.

'Hello, beautiful girl,' Max said the next morning when I arrived at his place and walked into his garage. We hugged and he stroked my hair. The storm had passed. The previous day still clung to me like a wet sweater, sagging and uncomfortable, but I didn't say anything about it, didn't want to spoil the new day, the sense of possibility that this one would be different.

And it *was* different.

We'd both adjusted our attitudes overnight. He was kind and patient. I tried to listen respectfully when he showed me how to use various tools: hand-planes of different sizes, an electric planer, the dropsaw. There were a hundred little instructions for each tool, most of them motivated by efficiency and safety: how to hold it, how to stand, when to squeeze the trigger, how to loop the power cord over my wrist to keep it out of the way, how to put the hand-planes down on the bench to avoid damaging their blades. It was different to the way Sophie worked. But Max was the one I was going to be working with; I had to learn his way, at least until I found my own. And I appreciated that he was taking the time to teach me.

We cut more than a dozen hardwood planks into slats for the chairs that day, planed them smooth and drilled holes in them ready to start screwing them into place, until we called it quits late in the afternoon, with high-fives. Well, Max's version of a high-five, which changed daily and could be anything from a slow hand-slide to a tickle with his fingers. That day the palm of his hand gently grazed mine and it made me smile.

It had been a smooth, productive day. But back at my place, I suddenly felt overcome by everything that hadn't been said. I lay on the cool concrete floor and cried. Underneath the satisfaction of learning new, practical things lay an old fear: of being dominated by someone else's worldview, of not feeling safe to be myself or do things my own way. It was a fear that could make me feel small, like a candle afraid of being outshone by the sun and forgetting its own different value.

I was afraid, too, of what it would be like living on Max's land after the build, in a tangle of debt and gratitude. This wasn't just about the build. This was about the place I would soon call home. So I lay on the floor, feeling torn. Part of me cooed reassuring words, tried to dilute the fear with reason, reminded me that this is what adventures feel like, especially at the beginning, while a persistent thought circled like a sea eagle riding a thermal, around and around and around: *How are we going to build a tiny together if we can't even make a couple of chairs?*

After those first two unsettled days, Max and I found a kind of equilibrium. I even had a small epiphany. The more comfortable I felt using various power tools – even the electric planer, a heavy, extremely noisy machine with a fast-spinning blade underneath – the more I could focus on what I was doing and the less I worried about doing it 'right'. My attention could let go of the *tool* in my hand and focus instead on the *task* at hand, and nothing else.

# Tiny

The day I finished my chair, I was leaning over its seat, holding the impact driver, when a few tears slipped past my safety glasses and dripped onto the timber slats I was screwing into place. I'd been working calmly, concentrating on what I was doing, but the ups and downs of the previous two weeks, mingled with apprehension about the build – our starting line was days away now – had caught up with me.

I put down the impact driver, took off my glasses and wiped my eyes. Max looked up from his own chair.

'What just happened?' I said, almost laughing. My emotional seas often obeyed a tidal flow of their own, one I was always trying to understand, but in that moment they didn't engulf me. I was able to watch them, not be washed away by them. Max noticed that, too.

'I have no idea, but I love you,' he said, enveloping me in a sawdusty hug.

We ended the day with what was to become my favourite part of every woodworking project: oiling the finished thing. As we brushed tung oil onto our chairs, the blackbutt slats began to change. It was like watching a Polaroid develop. Rusty reds, chocolate browns and the wood's natural knots and swirls, previously hidden by grime and sawdust, materialised before our eyes. I was still a rookie, still scared of the impact driver's jackhammer stutter and I'd broken a few screws just that morning while I was attaching the final slats to my chair, but compared to where I'd been two weeks earlier, this was progress. And one more step in the direction of my tiny.

⌂

An old ex-Army Land Rover pulled up in front of Max's place later that month, towing my brand-new trailer. We went out to meet the delivery driver, Gordo. Beside him sat Billy Ray, his Jack Russell terrier, looking every bit as thrilled to be there – after being on the road for two days – as I was to see my trailer.

As Gordo expertly reversed up Max's driveway, no easy feat with a trailer almost twice as long as his vehicle, a small crowd of neighbours and curious friends gathered to watch and to inspect the new arrival.

'It's big,' every one of them said.

It certainly was the biggest trailer I'd ever seen. And beautiful, in its own industrial way. But it looked small to me, too, because I was already wondering how my whole home – my kitchen and bathroom, the stairs to my bed loft, my couch and my desk and a life I couldn't quite envisage yet – was going to fit on top of it.

Later, after everyone had left, I clambered onto my new trailer. Standing in the afternoon sunlight slanting between the giant eucalypts along the western edge of Max's driveway, I imagined myself standing at my kitchen bench, looking out the window at these trees in just a few months' time, if all went well.

Max emerged from his house, climbed up beside me, put his arm around me.

'You OK?'

'Yeah.' I smiled, my eyes filling up. All day I'd been feeling it, a shining excitement too big to keep inside. The trailer was here. We were really doing this.

# PART 3
# BULDING

*'Nothing lasts, nothing is finished, nothing is perfect.'*
~ Richard R. Powell on the Japanese concept of *wabi-sabi*

Chapter 10

# A shaky start

Day one. A cool, sunny September morning. I arrived early at Max's place looking every bit the newbie in my new overalls, my toolbelt slung around my hips like a holster holding my new hammer and tape measure, my earmuffs and safety glasses. I'd also brought all my notes and plans in a shiny electric-purple (the only colour available) expanding file George had, understandably, christened 'Barbie's campervan'. On my feet were the only bits of my outfit with any 'I belong here' cred, my scuffed old Blundstone boots.

Max met me at the trailer with a hug, his workwear more casual than mine: a paint-splattered business shirt (long-sleeved, for sun protection), shorts, sneakers and a much-used toolbelt. Then George arrived, dressed like the building version of a rock star with nothing to prove: faded Che Guevara T-shirt, ripped board shorts and rubber thongs. I'd soon learn that he wore shoes and safety gear only when absolutely necessary.

After a brief planning chat in the driveway – the trailer was parked next to Max's garage – we took our places, like characters in a play. Act 1, Scene 1.

The previous weekend I'd waterproofed several sheets of marine ply with multiple coats of bitumen paint, black on black on black, feeling like

Daniel in *The Karate Kid* painting Mr Miyagi's fence. It had been slow, tedious work with long pauses between coats to allow them to dry, but I'd felt glad to finally be doing something.

Now we had to lay those sheets on the trailer and fix them in place; they would seal the bottom of my tiny from the elements and, when in transit, from any water, mud or gravel that might splash up from the road.

Simple. Straightforward. I was a jangle of nerves. Thoughts and questions rushed into my head. *Where was I supposed to stand, what was I supposed to do, should I be doing it like this?* I took a few deep breaths and commando-crawled under the trailer, armed with a tube of black Sikaflex adhesive and a caulking gun. My mission: to seal the gaps where dozens of steel tabs (part of the tiny house building method we were using) poked up from the trailer through slots we'd cut in the marine ply.

Meanwhile, George and Max clambered around above me, on top of the trailer, making floor joists and bolting them to those steel tabs, chatting as they worked. I didn't know it then but this would become the soundtrack of our build, for the first couple of months at least. There was no talkback radio, no classic rock, just this baritone banter of two men who clearly enjoyed working together, an all-day riff punctuated by cups of tea and a brief lunch, about blues or the news or whatever they had to do next, sometimes in funny voices for their own, and my, amusement.

'Stupid is as stupid does, sir!' Max liked to say, in his best Forrest Gump accent.

I didn't have much experience of these things, but it seemed a gentlemanly building site. Even profanities were rare, muttered only out of frustration or for comic effect.

'Loui, Georgie just said the F-word,' Max said with mock primness that first afternoon, leaning over the edge of the trailer to grin down at me.

Lying on my back under the trailer, nose to steel, I smiled up at him. 'Naughty Georgie,' I said, playing my part.

By the end of the day, my hands were aching from squeezing the stiff trigger of the caulking gun, my face and arms were covered in smears of sticky black Sikaflex, my new overalls were grimy with dirt and gravel, and I couldn't have been happier. After six months of designing and decisions, waiting and planning, we were building at last. *This was going to be fun. What had I been worried about?*

The next day, things weren't quite so free and easy. Before we could start putting down the floor of my tiny, George and Max needed to know how big the shower recess would be and how many kitchen cabinets I wanted, how deep they'd be and how far they would extend along the western side...

It was my first lesson in how building works: good builders, experienced builders, are constantly thinking ahead, checking that what they're working on today will connect with what they'll be working on tomorrow, next week or in a month's time. Because everything's connected. It's true in nature – as American naturalist John Muir said, 'When we try to pick out anything by itself, we find it hitched to everything else in the universe' – and apparently it's true in building, too.

What this meant in practice was that – surprise! – I had to make some big decisions that first week, decisions I hadn't been expecting so soon and wasn't ready to make, about things I hadn't thought about yet, or ever. Learning that everything was connected only made it worse. What if I made a wrong call on something early in the build and caused a cascade of mistakes that couldn't be undone and my whole tiny house project ended in disaster?

Before Max, the last person I was in a relationship with, back when I lived in Sydney, was a Kiwi mountain man who led hiking and cycling trips in New Zealand for a living. An outdoor guide with a craggy face and a smile that could make you walk anywhere, he used to tell me that the first day of any multi-day trip was a 'shakedown' day, built into the schedule to allow everyone to settle into the group and get used to their gear and the new routine.

Week one of our build was our 'shakedown' week. We made some progress – subfloor done, floor joists bolted into place and we'd started on the flooring – but mostly we were finding our way into the project, figuring out how to work together, learning strategies that would carry us through the coming months.

On top of all that, I'd been studying tiny houses for a few years, had done a tiny-building workshop (twice!), had watched a thousand tiny tours and now had a few woodworking skills – but I didn't know a thing about building. George, on the other hand, had forty-odd years of experience as a professional builder – but had never built a tiny house. And between us was Max: my partner and George's best friend.

This dynamic first reared its head after lunch on Friday. We were working on the bathroom floor and Max was dabbing Sikaflex on the tops of the floor joists, to glue down the plywood floor so it wouldn't squeak when someone walked on it. But I was worried; Sikaflex is quite a toxic adhesive and we'd been using a lot of it. Also, it had been a long day and an intense first week.

'Why are we using Sikaflex for this, again?' I asked Max, not knowing which of my three building-site hard hats to wear in that moment: apprentice, project manager or owner.

George was standing beside him, preparing to lay down the first sheet of plywood.

'Because this is how it's done and it's been DONE this way for, like, a HUNDRED years,' he snapped.

I felt stunned. I'm a naturally curious person. When I travel, I'm always the one taking more notes and asking more questions than I really need to, because my mind just likes to wonder, and learn, particularly when it's not otherwise engaged. George did not know this about me. And it's possible I'd already asked more than a few questions that day about all sorts of things, partly out of excitement, which he possibly wasn't used to. But he had made it abundantly clear I'd asked one question too many.

I suddenly, desperately, missed my travel writing life, where I could ask questions to my heart's content, where caring about every little detail was a good thing. This was a short, sharp reminder that building is not like that, at least not all the time, and definitely not when someone is trying to get something done and finish up for the day and they just want to bloody do it without some rookie pestering them. I felt like a silly girl, disturbing the men while they did Important Things, on *my* house.

I retreated, and found something inconsequential to do while Max and George finished the bathroom floor.

Later, before George left for the day, I walked over to where he and Max were packing up their tools beside the trailer. I wanted to smooth the ruffled air between us. It had been a micro-argument, about a tiny bit of the tiny house, but we were all going to be working together for a while and I didn't want any first-week awkwardness or annoyances to fester into something more serious. Plus, it was my project; I felt responsible for keeping our workplace harmonious.

'Um, George,' I said, resting my hands on the edge of the trailer. He stopped what he was doing to listen. 'I just want to say thanks for being patient with me this week and for explaining so much.' I was half-smiling, quite nervous. 'I know it's only our first week and we're all getting used to working together, but I'm sorry for asking so many questions. I didn't mean to question *you* or what you're doing or how you're doing it. I'm just curious and I want to learn.'

George nodded, gave me a tight-lipped smile. 'I appreciate that, thanks Lou. We're trying to teach you.'

I decided to curb my curiosity from then on, as much as I could. I didn't have to know *everything* about my tiny and I could learn a lot by watching and listening. Still, something about our air-clearing didn't feel complete.

'That was a good thing you said to Georgie this afternoon,' Max said that evening while we talked about the day over bowls of pasta at his place. It was only then that I realised George hadn't apologised for losing his temper. But when I mentioned that to Max, he leapt to his friend's defence: George was having to make a lot of changes to the way he usually worked to do this job, he was helping us as a favour, I should cut him some slack.

An old song started playing in my head, one I'd been hearing for a long time, since before I'd even met Max: *Don't make the men angry*. Along with: *Men aren't responsible for their own emotions*. That's women's work, the song said. *Keep the peace, keep house, keep smiling*. That's what Mum did, what she'd learned to do. I'd learned, too, to watch Dad's moods, to adjust my behaviour to the emotional weather, stay under the radar, not make things worse. When he was impatient, I kept my distance. When he was angry, I replayed what I'd said or done, believing, as children do, it'd been my fault. Even when he was playful, I kept an eye out for squalls on the horizon. Expectations were always unspoken, like landmines waiting to be stepped on.

I'd turned this over in my mind so many times, tried to understand it, talked to therapists about it, and still it haunted me, the sense that I had to read the signs, and others' minds, keep everyone happy. I always found this tricky in intimate relationships, and in my relationship with Max, knowing who was responsible for what. When something happened, which part came from me and my stuff, which part came from him and his, and what was just the dance of this amorphous, ever-changing 'us' we'd created?

Early the next morning, Max and I drove to the beach for a swim. We needed to do something fun together. But as he was parking his van beside the surf club, I made a mistake. I asked him about some timber he'd bought at Bunnings, our nearest mega-hardware store, a couple of days earlier. I'd seen it in the driveway before we'd left, noticed that he'd bought a different type from the one we'd agreed on.

'Hey, how come you bought the treated timber studs and not the untreated ones we talked about?' We'd both wanted to minimise the use of chemicals on the build and had agreed that un-termite-proofed studs would be fine for my house frame.

'Didn't think about it.' He turned off the ignition.

'It was on that list I gave you.' Keeping my tone light.

'Didn't look at the list.'

'Oh.'

He turned to look at me. 'Why do you have to react to everything?'

In that moment, I didn't care about the kind of studs he'd bought. I cared about the way he spoke to me, the hostility in his voice. I didn't understand what was going on underneath his words, but I didn't ask and wasn't sure I wanted to know. I wanted us to be able to weather a simple misunderstanding without capsizing. I wanted us to drop our defences, run into the water and wash away the angst between us.

'Let's have a swim,' I said, getting out of the car. Walking across the soft sand to the water's edge, turning to see that he wasn't coming, wading in, feeling the sea smooth me all over, waiting for him. Walking back to the car. He was still there, staring at the sea, listening to music. We drove home in silence.

Back at his place, I didn't join him for breakfast. Instead I took a cup of tea and my tape measure outside and climbed onto the trailer to do something useful: figure out the exact length of my kitchen bench. This would determine where my front door would go, so we could start building the wall frames the following week. Because everything's connected.

It was the first time I'd been alone on our build site and it made me realise how focused I'd been all week on Max and George and what they were doing and where I fit in, how out of my depth I'd felt. But standing on the trailer that Saturday morning, figuring things out at my own pace, in my own way, settled me. I did belong here.

After a while, Max walked over from his house. What had happened earlier hung in the air, ignored by us both. But when he saw me measuring, he fetched a couple of wooden stools from his verandah and, without saying a word, placed them on top of the makeshift plywood floor. I smiled my thanks and we sat side by side at my imaginary kitchen bench, looking out an imaginary window, trying to start the day again, listening to the birds in the trees all around us.

Chapter 11

# Reality check

A few years ago, I did an all-woman trek in the Sierra Nevada mountains in California. Our two female guides were ultra-experienced climbers and mountaineers – one of them did search-and-rescue work in Yosemite, the other had climbed Everest – and my fellow hikers came from all over America. Some were seasoned outdoorswomen; some had never put up a tent on their own. We were all strangers to each other.

Two days into the two-week trip, as the rocky trail gained altitude, I noticed something. Whenever someone started falling behind, from fatigue or the increasingly thin air or because she was just travelling a bit more slowly than the rest of us that day, someone else in the group would suggest we all take a break. We were still getting to know each other, still learning each other's names, but a rest stop would spontaneously happen, without our guides having to make the call. A shady spot would be chosen and we'd all take off our packs, sit down, sip water, pass around some chocolate – and stay there until the last to arrive felt revived enough to carry on.

There was never any mention of 'helping' anyone else; that was too top-down. This was intuitive and inclusive and felt completely natural, though I hadn't experienced it on other hikes. That sense of care and camaraderie percolated through other parts of the trip, too: route-planning, setting up camp, preparing dinner. We were all capable enough individually, but on that trip we learned we could do more – and have more fun doing it – if we worked together. And at the end of those two weeks, after travelling through that rugged mountainscape with these women, sharing more than just a physical experience, this unconsciously became my gold standard for 'how to do practical things with other people'.

Max and I spent that first weekend apart, to regroup. It was a relief to not think about the relationship for a couple of days. I took long walks on the beach, barefoot in jeans and a woollen jumper, letting icy southerly winds blow through me – and thought about the build instead.

I'd been feeling a gnawing sense of being left out. Instead of the three of us working together, Max and George were a team of two, moving fast, getting things done. They were used to working together, seemed to almost read each other's minds about what to do next and they had an unblemished history of shared good times, something Max and I certainly didn't have.

I didn't expect them to work at my pace or include me in every step of the build. But I didn't want them to march on to the summit without me either. Something had to change, something in me.

Sometimes, during the build, I'd read or hear about other women, most of them as inexperienced as I was, building their tiny houses single-handedly and I'd feel another kind of 'build envy'. What these women were doing looked tough, time-consuming and *honest*. When they finished their builds, they'd be able to say, 'I made this.'

I couldn't help comparing myself to them. Some of them were younger and fitter than I was, but some of them weren't. I told myself my situation was different. It would have been foolish to refuse Max and George's help on principle, just for the satisfaction of saying I'd done the build on my own, the 'hard way' (for one thing, I knew I'd have a finished tiny much sooner if I worked with them) but there was a part of me that wanted to do exactly that, to prove something, maybe just to myself.

But, do we ever really do anything by ourselves? We're all standing on the shoulders of those who have walked before us, broken ground for us. And even solo builders need help sometimes. Besides, doing things alone was my default mode. I was used to working and travelling alone, I often surfed and went camping alone, and I'd been living alone for a few years. Maybe the 'hard way' for me, this time, was *not* doing the build on my own.

That weekend, I did an internal reality check. I needed to let go of my ideas of how this build should be, and my gold standard from that hike in the Sierras. If I wanted Max and George's help, I needed to *let them* help me. George was only going to be around for the first part of the build anyway; after that, Max and I could tackle the interior fit-out together and find a rhythm that worked for us. In the meantime, I vowed to embrace my rookie-apprentice role more, by being content with minor jobs, driving to the hardware store for supplies, and tidying the worksite at the end of each day. I reminded myself that every job, big or small, was moving me towards my new home.

I was starting to accept that anxiety was probably going to shadow me for much of the build, but I wanted to learn how to make (good) decisions quickly and without getting flustered. So I called my friend Jodi. She's a welder and an artist and used to standing her ground in male-dominated workplaces; as psychology nerds, we often talked about relationships and gender dynamics and why people do the things we do.

'Just say, "Give me five minutes and I'll get back to you",' she said, matter of factly. Five minutes to clear my head, do some quick research and thinking in peace, before returning, confident in my decision. As a strategy, it was beautifully simple.

'And remember,' she added, 'this is your project. You have a right to be there.'

By Monday morning of our second week, I felt more relaxed about everything. Max and George seemed more at ease, too, after our 'shakedown' week. We made a plan for the week – finish the hardwood flooring and start making the timber frame – and Max wrote a list of 'Loui's jobs' on a scrap of plywood. Things were looking up. Until I told him about one final decision I'd made on the weekend.

When we'd first started talking about the build, before any of us really knew how much work was involved, George had offered his help as a favour to Max, who was going to repay him by working on George's house later. After that first week, that didn't seem right. Much as I was trying to keep to a budget, I needed to pay George, out of a sense of fairness and to help clarify our working relationship; I was planning to ask him for his hourly rate that morning. But first I wanted to let Max know.

'I already told Georgie you'd pay him,' he said, while we were laying out the tools we were going to need that day.

'When?'

He shrugged. 'Few days ago.' The day he and George had driven to the hardware store together. He'd known about this for four days? It was another speed bump that, in a more secure relationship, could have been resolved with a 'Sorry I didn't tell you earlier' or an 'I'm glad we're on the same page'. But we hadn't started the build in a good place and misunderstandings kept finding their way into our interactions, like salt sprinkled on a wound that wasn't healing, that couldn't heal. I felt constantly off-balance – and that that was my problem. *If I felt disappointed, I must have expected too much.* I tried to be flexible, give Max the benefit of the doubt, but below the waterline of everything between us was something I wasn't yet ready to believe: we were in trouble.

⌂

That second week, I started doing something else to steady myself. It began as a small experiment, a bit of whimsy, a kiss blown in the direction of a future me. I wrote words in secret places on the trailer, with whatever was within reach. Starting with *Love* finger-painted on the plywood subfloor with Sikaflex, that goopy black adhesive.

With that first simple word, something sparked awake inside me. I began carrying a blue texta in my toolbelt (the Sikaflex was too messy) and scrawled more secret words at opportune moments, small and uncertainly at first, on that blank plywood canvas between the floor joists. *Peace. Harmony. Kindness. Joy.*

The words gathered themselves into lines, phrases, then whole sentences from books and poems I loved, like 'Keep close to nature's heart and break clear away once in a while and climb a mountain or spend a week in the woods. Wash your spirit clean' by John Muir, and 'Do not try to save the whole world or do anything grandiose. Instead create a clearing in the dense forest of your life and wait there patiently until the song that is yours alone to sing falls into your own cupped hands' by Martha Postlethwaite.

I didn't tell Max or George what I was doing or why – I barely knew myself – and they didn't ask, which was a relief.

When the floor insulation had to go in, a blanket of fluffy white batts covered my secret words like a fresh dump of snow. Just before we started laying the hardwood floor, I lifted a corner of one of those fluffy white squares and drew one last thing: an old-fashioned love heart pierced by an arrow, my initials at its feathered end and Max's at the pointy tip. I called him over to show him – before it disappeared forever – and handed him the texta, a silent invitation. He wrote his reply: *The world is a better place with your love in it.*

We nailed down the floorboards – blackbutt tongue-and-groove planks Max had given me, left over from re-flooring his own house years ago – sealing the underfloor area, plank by plank, like the lid of a time capsule. My secret words would never see daylight again. And although they served no practical purpose, writing them seemed important. Not just to quieten my mind amid the new-girl whirl of everything, but as a small act of rebellion, a way to reclaim the build, reconnect with what we were doing on my terms, and it reassured me that something inside me had known to do this, something I could trust.

Chapter 12

# Three dimensional

To a novice, complicated tasks can look implausibly simple. You don't have the experience or knowledge to understand all the variables, all that needs to be done, all that can go wrong. But in the case of framing a tiny house, it really was simple: make the frames for each of the four walls, stand them up, then bolt them to each other and to the trailer.

The first step was to mark up the bottom plate, which involved making pencil marks on a rectangle of treated pine (the bottom plate) attached to the edges of my trailer, which would guide us in making the frames that would sit on top of it.

Armed with my hand-drawn plans, (flat) builder's pencils and tape measures, George and I spent a sunny Tuesday afternoon doing a slow circumambulation of the trailer, stopping every few steps so he could ask me questions. *How wide is that window? How far is the front door from that end wall? What's the vertical distance between those two windows?* It was like a tiny house pop quiz and it surprised me – possibly George too – that I had a ready answer for every one of his questions.

Despite that brief blip at the end of our first week, George and I worked well together. He knew what he was doing, had done this thousands of times, on regular-sized houses. And I, apparently, knew my tiny house, inside out and back to front, after all the long nights I'd spent hunched over the coffee table at my place drawing and redrawing it from every possible angle.

Months later, when the tiny was almost finished, friends would pop in to see it and often ask detailed questions about the build, because they were thinking about building a tiny themselves or were just interested in how so much could fit into such a small space. And I'd surprise myself all over again by being able to reel off measurements and materials and say what we'd done and how we'd done it and recite a hundred other things I'd learned about building, like some kind of tiny house savant.

I was quietly ecstatic that the first house plans I'd ever drawn had actually worked. And I didn't feel the slightest flutter of anxiety that day. I didn't second-guess what I was doing or what I said. I didn't feel confused or insecure. All my attention was laser-focused on what we were doing, which calmed me, and meant I wasn't so ruffled by the changing winds of Max's affections. He'd been working in the garage all afternoon, keeping to himself, letting George and me do our thing, but he wandered over as we were putting the last pencil marks on the last corner of the bottom plate.

'All your hard work's paid off, Loui,' Max said. I didn't need it that day, but it felt good to have his stamp of approval.

Over the next few days, we made the timber frame to put on top of that marked-up bottom plate. It all happened quickly, but with great care. It's easier to change things on a timber frame than on, say, a steel one – because bits of wood can be pulled apart, whereas welded steel is welded forever, unless you cut the joins with an angle grinder – but mistakes cause delays. We had to get each frame right the first time.

I loved this part of the build. For one thing, we were a crew of three again. Starting on one of the long sides, George and I would double-check the numbers we'd written on the bottom plate, working from one end to the other, then he'd translate them into the vertical plane. He seemed to *see* the unbuilt wall in front of him, with all its studs (vertical lengths of bright-blue treated pine) and blocks (shorter horizontal bits between the studs, also adorably called noggins) and spaces for all the windows and the front door.

Then he'd call out a batch of numbers to Max, who would immediately cut the lengths of pine we needed at his table-mounted dropsaw, set up in the sun next to the trailer, and I'd run the cut lengths over to George, who would nail them to each other using his temperamental nail-gun. Sometimes George would tell me the measurements for the next section and I'd write '550, 530, 440' on a scrap of sky-blue wood and give it to Max like a waitress handing a ticket to a short-order cook.

'Loui!'

'Yes, chef!'

'Is this a five or an eight?'

'A five, chef!'

It was high energy and fun, the kind of fun that emerges naturally from something you're doing, just because you're enjoying doing it. And by the end of the week, there was a stack of bright-blue house frames – each one looking like a dozen empty picture frames stuck together – lying in the driveway, ready to be attached to each other.

The following Monday was the moment of truth. The day we'd find out if our painstakingly made frames fit together, if all the windows lined up, if my measurements had been as accurate as they needed to be.

We lifted the heavy frames onto the trailer, one by one, and stood them upright. While Max and I held the first two at right angles to each other, George attached them to the bottom plate, accompanied by the periodic 'ker-pow!' of his nail-gun. We did the same for the third frame, then the fourth, until all four sides of my tiny were in place. Then George added a few diagonal cross-braces to make sure none of the walls could fall over before we got the roof on.

The final step was mine to do: bolting the wall studs in each corner to long steel tabs sticking up from the trailer, with a socket wrench. I'd never even used a socket wrench before, but Max showed me what to do and I just did it.

When I'd finished, I jumped down off the trailer, high-fived Max and George and turned to look at this skeletal blue thing we'd made. All the windows *did* line up. The corners all met neatly. Everything looked just as it should. We celebrated with cups of tea and date scones I'd baked early that morning, sitting on upturned milk crates in the leafy shade of a blackbean tree. I couldn't seem to stop smiling. Or quite believe that in the space of an hour on a sunny Monday morning the tiny house I'd been thinking about for so long had become a three-dimensional structure I could walk around in. Things were getting real again.

Chapter 13

# Choosing to stay

As the tiny changed shape in those first few weeks, Max and I, carried along on an ever-flowing river of jobs to do and the excitement of the build progressing, found ourselves getting along without even trying. He'd give me little squeezes, speak in weird accents to make me laugh and take pictures of me as we worked. One afternoon in the hardware store – we'd become one of those couples that browsed Bunnings on Sunday afternoons, earnestly discussing home construction and deliberating over kitchen taps – he apologised for speaking sharply to me, something I hadn't even noticed.

We had date nights, too, every Wednesday, which involved *not* talking about the build or tiny houses over dinner at his place or mine, both of us too exhausted to actually dress up and go out, before curling up on the couch in front of a movie. *This is home*, I'd think, feeling the warmth of his body against mine. *This is why we're together, why we've weathered the storms we've been through, for times like these.*

Strange how those good times, when everything is steady-as-she-goes, can fool you into thinking everything is OK. That you'd imagined or exaggerated the bad times. That those times when you'd felt anxious or alone were exceptions, not the rule. *Every relationship cycles through connection, disconnection and reconnection. This is normal. We're normal.*

Until there's a shift, subtle as a puff of wind, so subtle you doubt it, doubt yourself. You misunderstood. You were being silly, over-sensitive. But no. The lighthouse beam that had bathed you in goodness and safety for the last little while sweeps past you, to shine on something else, someone else. And you're in the shadows again, wondering what happened and when the light is coming back, and you realise. *This isn't normal.*

Halfway through the week when the frames went up, Max and I went to see Sean, a couples' counsellor we'd been having sessions with, sporadically, for a couple of months.

Max had been distant for a few days and we didn't speak on the half-hour drive there. I felt nervous about what might come up once we started talking to Sean, but I was looking forward to that, too. It was always better to know. And I felt safe and at ease with Sean. In our first session, he'd seen the love immediately, seen how committed Max and I were to each other, told us that was worth fighting for. Sean would know what to do, I thought, to help us bridge the growing chasm between us.

'How about we start today with each of you saying something you appreciate about the other,' Sean said as soon as Max and I got settled in the two pale-blue armchairs facing him. I kicked off my sandals and tucked my feet under me.

There was a pause, as if we were deciding who would go first.

'I can't do it,' Max said. I turned to look at him. He seemed deflated, all the love gone out of him.

'That's OK,' Sean said, unfazed. 'Lou, do you want to have a go?'

'Um, OK. I like... Max's playfulness and that he cares about people and the world.' It felt good to say even these small things, made me realise that although I'd been thanking Max and praising his work on the build every day, my head had been full of unspoken complaints lately, and thoughts about how different I wanted things to be between us.

Max didn't seem to have heard what I'd said. 'For the first time in our relationship, I'm not sure we can make this work,' he said, flatly, not looking at me. At first, I was surprised: he'd *never* thought it might not work out between us? Some days I'd have that thought three times before breakfast.

But he was serious, and didn't seem willing or able to engage, to change gear, even with Sean's gentle coaxing. Whenever Sean asked how he felt, Max said what he *thought*, and all his thoughts had barbs on them, aimed at me. I listened, trying to understand, feeling myself sink into the cushions of my chair. I wasn't sure if we could make this work either, or if I wanted to. I wasn't afraid of losing Max. I was afraid of losing myself if I stayed with him.

⌂

I don't know when it started, my ambivalence towards intimate relationships, the sense that something was wrong with me because I didn't feel the way I thought I should feel, the way I wanted to feel, when I was with someone I liked.

My first relationships with boys were easy and fun. That sweet, magnetic pull towards someone, when a glance in your direction could make your insides do cartwheels, and holding hands filled you up so much you wouldn't stop smiling for hours. The litmus test of compatibility: do we like being around each other? It was all so simple.

And I could fall in love. I loved the blurring of boundaries, the letting in, the surrender to another's orbit, how it felt to hold someone's attention, and be held by it. The first time, I was eighteen and we were both in our first year at the same university. An engineering student, Jack was shy and smart with gentle hands and white-blonde hair. Within days of meeting we became a couple, walking to lectures together, listening to Midnight Oil albums on the floor of his bedroom, windsurfing on weekends with our friends and stealing moments of intimacy after parties, at my front door, trying not to wake my parents, or in the front seat of his mum's hatchback. I'd fallen under the no-sex-before-marriage spell, not uncommon at the time where I grew up, but we did our best to work around that, and the gear stick.

I could do breakups too, and often stayed friends with my exes. With Jack, breaking up was as tender and undramatic as our relationship had been; we sat on the grass under a tree behind the maths building one afternoon, three years after we'd got together, and agreed in very few words that it was over. We hadn't hurt each other. Neither of us fancied anyone else. Things had just run their course. I don't even remember crying.

Eventually I got over my virgin phase and began my long-distance phase. The more nomadic a guy was, the more I liked him. I loved the months-long separations as much as the euphoric reunions. My female friends couldn't understand why I didn't want someone around all the time, but, to me, I had the best of both worlds: freedom *and* someone to love.

Looking back now, I think having unconventional relationships was a way to love someone, and be loved, that made sense to me. But at the time this was all I knew: I wanted intimacy, and was beginning to fear it. I never expected a guy to make me happy. I just didn't want being in a relationship to make me miserable and that's often what would happen. Things would start out well, then something would change. I seemed to lose, or give up, some vital part of myself to the person I was with, to the relationship, until I just didn't want to be with him anymore. So this became my secret wish: to be with someone – someone I could trust and talk to and share the whole beautiful mess of life and love with – *and* be with myself.

When I met Max, I hadn't been in a relationship for almost four years, wasn't looking for anyone, felt comfortable in my own skin. With him I felt more loved and more certain of my love for another than I had in a long time. And when I started to lose myself, the way I always did, he was understanding. He loved that I wanted to talk about things, to look at what was going on inside. I felt brave and strong and sure of us.

But as the honeymoon of our relationship began to fade, I noticed things that made me uneasy. Sometimes, after we'd surfed together, he'd disappear into a friend's house for a cup of tea without telling me, while I waited beside the car for him, wondering where he was. A few months into our relationship, everything still fresh-faced between us, he booked a flight to Europe and announced that he was going rock climbing with some mates for five months. Although I wasn't into long-distance relationships anymore, I understood the pull of travel. Still, it hurt. *I was always wishing I could take him on my work trips; didn't he want to travel with me too?* One summer afternoon, soon after he got back, I arrived a few minutes late to meet him at the lake for a swim and found him preparing to leave; he was going to a friend's place for dinner, something he hadn't mentioned earlier.

'I'm not going to put my life on hold for you,' he said through his open window, driving off. He was gone before I could say, 'I never asked you to.'

He had more friends than anyone I'd ever known, and was extraordinarily good at keeping in touch with them all. I'd liked this about him, that he was always helping people out, remembering birthdays, driving friends to medical appointments, running errands for elderly 'uncles' and 'aunties' in town. But it made our relationship feel crowded sometimes.

On the beach one wintry day, after a long and heartfelt talk, we went for a walk that turned into a run. The sea breeze ruffled my hair and we yelped as we jumped off small sandhills and splashed through the shallows and played at chasing each other and I felt as happy as a puppy. He looked happy too. I loved us like this. Then he ran ahead and turned around to say something, his eyes smiling.

'You know what I love about Kev? He *loves* doing stuff like this! I love how playful he is!'

Had I heard him properly? The man I loved had been running beside me, thinking about one of his mates. I tried to understand: it was a momentary thought, minds wander, it was good that he wanted to share what he was thinking. But he'd left me again, and we'd only just reconnected. I went quiet, afraid to say why I felt off-balance. I was sure he'd see it as unreasonable. Part of *me* saw it as unreasonable. I wanted to not feel so rocked when he praised his friends, but I felt eclipsed by his love for them. Even when we were alone, their presence in his life seemed to leave less room for me.

I had friends in secure relationships who couldn't really fathom, if I happened to mention an incident like this, how it could so unglue me. Or they'd ask why I didn't leave Max, if I felt so insecure in the relationship so often. My only explanation was that when it was good it was great – and

I'd never been in a stable, happy relationship; I didn't even know what that kind of love would feel like.

Instead I'd learned to look for signs and symptoms that this person was losing interest in me or we weren't right together after all or it was going to end, soon and in a way that would hurt. I turned experience into rules to live by: relationships are hard, you have to work at love, nothing lasts forever. And underneath all that was this: I arrived at every relationship pre-loaded with insecurity from the difficult relationship I'd had with Dad most of my life, particularly after Mum died, one in which I felt loved but not really seen, understood or even liked. I saw in Max some of the qualities I'd found challenging in Dad, but part of me believed that being with someone like this would finally heal the wounds that had been stopping me from feeling safe and content in a relationship.

It felt like my last chance to love and be loved. No matter what happened between Max and me, how much things hurt, it was all grist for the mill, a way to learn and grow towards freedom *and* someone to love, at the same time, in the same place. The obstacles on the path *are* the path leading you home. I wanted this relationship to be the one that would finally break my pattern of running from love. I wanted to stay.

⌂

As I listened to Max tell his side of things that day in Sean's room, it sounded upside down. He seemed to be saying all the hard things were happening to *him*, through no fault of his own. And with Sean listening and empathising with him, I became untethered from my own perspective. *Were things really as Max said they were? Was I just not seeing the situation clearly?* I understood that a therapist can't take sides. But it overwhelmed me, when I was already feeling overlooked and underheard on a regular basis. A flood of feelings, too many to name or note, tumbled down on me from a great height. I leaned forward, held my head in my hands. I was disappearing again, barrelling along a tunnel, too fast, out of control, unable to stop or rein myself in. *The way you see things doesn't matter, what you feel doesn't matter. You don't matter.*

A sound broke through, Sean's voice, gentle, asking what was happening for me. I looked up, unfolded myself, tried to explain.

'This is what it feels like. When I feel hurt or upset about something that happens between us, that's my problem to deal with. That's OK, I know I have to take responsibility for my feelings and I'm trying to do that. But when Max is upset about something, that's somehow my problem too, because, as he sees it, I've done something wrong and his reaction, however extreme, is justified and somehow I deserve it. Whatever happens, I'm the one who's wrong, I'm the problem.'

I felt cornered, and alone. Max seemed far, far away.

But Sean was right there, understanding, holding what I'd said, not judging. I took some deep breaths. My body started to calm down.

In the last minutes of our session, Max placed his right hand on the padded arm of my chair, beside my left arm. I looked at his hand, felt the longing in it. And my own fear, of wading in again, being rejected or found to be wrong in some new and unexpected way.

I looked at Sean. 'It doesn't feel safe to take his hand.'

'What's the minimum you could do?' he said.

I touched one of Max's fingers then looked up and saw tears on his cheeks and the person behind them, *my person*, and everything inside me softened, surrendered, and I put my whole hand on his. Contact.

It was time to leave. We all stood up. There were hugs.

'Don't break up in the next two weeks, OK?' Sean said, warmly, as he opened the door. He had faith in us, that we could get through this.

Outside, Max and I held hands as we walked back to his van.

'Let's stay like this,' I said. He wiped the tears from my face and we put our arms around each other and stood like that for a long time on the footpath of the busy street.

Back at his place, both too wrung out to do anything else, we climbed the ladder to his sleeping loft. It was only four in the afternoon, but we fell into a deep, exhausted sleep, skin to skin, our legs and arms wrapped around each other like vines.

Chapter 14

# Holding on

The closeness we'd felt after the couples' session faded fast. My skin seemed made of paper, easily torn by things Max said and did. Meanwhile he seemed in a constant state of irritation, communicated with me on a 'need to know' basis. When we did talk about something to do with the build, it was as if there was a scrambler between us, encrypting our words to stop us understanding each other.

By the end of that week, he was barely speaking to me at all.

We'd had another wobble the previous day when he'd criticised me in front of George. I'd tried to shrug it off at the time, but when George left for the day I told Max his words had hurt and, remembering how close we'd felt after seeing Sean, hoped we could talk about it. Max didn't want to talk about it. Instead he retreated into himself, out of my reach, and stayed that way for the whole next day.

It was just before sunset and we were standing in the driveway after George had gone home, the first time we'd been alone all day. I asked him what was going on.

He'd been putting up with this for *three years*, he said. *Making allowances*. 'I'm not going to take any more of your crap.' I didn't understand. What crap? He didn't say.

Part of me felt relieved he was letting his feelings out, letting me in. This was real. I could handle this, I could listen, I could see that he was hurting.

'I can't do this anymore,' he said, his mouth a straight line.

I reached over to touch his arm. He pulled away.

'If this goes on, I'm going to tell George to pull the pin,' he said.

He knew I wouldn't be able to find another builder at short notice to help with this structural stage of the build. Without George, progress would grind to a halt. And did Max mean *he'd* pull out of the build, too? He'd always said that no matter what happened between us, we would build my tiny on his land, together, but I wasn't sure of anything anymore.

'It's OK,' I said, trying to reassure us both, trying to see the wounded boy behind the angry man. Failing on both counts.

'Just fuck off home,' he said, and walked away.

I didn't sleep much that night. Got up in the dark the next morning, drove to the beach, sat in my car waiting for the sun to burn away the darkness, needing a reminder that the Earth was still turning.

The sea looked inviting. I thought a surf might clear my head, so I paddled out and sat on my board. No one else was out. A few dolphins swam underneath me, but even they couldn't reach me. Because sometimes being in the sea doesn't change how you feel; it just makes everything else fall away so you feel it more. I caught a wave in and walked across the road to the lake, left my surfboard on the grassy bank and waded into the tea-black water, let it swallow me. This was a woman's place once, the Bundjalung people say. A deep, dark body of water encircled by paperbarks standing guard. I'd always felt safe there.

I kept to myself that weekend, didn't see anyone, didn't go anywhere. On Sunday night, a message from Max: he'd picked up some timber, donated by one of our friends. It seemed the build was still on.

With George away the following week, Max and I took a couple of days off, to let the dust settle. Still, driving to his place on Wednesday, I felt anxiety tie knots in my stomach while my head ran through possible scenarios, trying to prepare me for the unexpected.

I found him dozing on a big black armchair on his deck in the sun. He smiled me over to him, invited me to join him on the chair. I was wary, but it felt good to have his arms around me. And when we started to talk, we didn't argue. He didn't remember threatening to tell George to stop work if things didn't change between us, reassured me that he would keep his word: I could build my tiny at his place, no matter what.

'How about this,' I said. 'We could put the relationship on hold and keep doing the build as friends. What do you think?'

'Yeah,' he said, pulling me close. Funny how taking all the pressure off suddenly makes breaking up seem quite unnecessary.

That afternoon and over the next couple of days, we worked together on a few small jobs as if we really were 'just friends'. Of course, we were playing at something we couldn't sustain. There was too much energy between us. So we tried another date night, our first in weeks, at my place this time, the usual routine: dinner, movie, bed, love dialled up all the way. This is how it goes. When it's bad, you can't speak to each other; when it's good, you don't want to rock the boat.

I lay in the boat and let it carry me away.

Chapter 15

# Bracing and blessing

Underneath the rollercoaster of us, the tiny was making steady progress, changing its look on a regular basis. At the start of our second month, it changed again.

It happened like this. Once the frame was up, we had to attach sheets of bracing ply – very thin plywood used to 'brace' the walls before the cladding went on – to the outside of the entire structure. Because the bracing ply was so thin, we couldn't use nails to fix it in place; the heads of the nails would have gone right through it. It was time to purchase my First Ever Power Tool.

My new black staple gun looked disturbingly like an actual gun, so I was relieved to learn that it fired staples only when firmly pressed against a hard surface. Also, unlike a real gun, it wasn't cordless: it had to be hooked up to George's bright yellow compressor (a small round-bellied tank on wheels) with a long rubber hose, adding a new level of difficulty to climbing ladders. And it was so heavy my wrists ached when I had to hold it up for too long. Still, I loved my staple gun. Mainly because, standing at the top of an extension ladder, wearing my overalls, my earmuffs and my safety glasses, my toolbelt loaded with clips of staples, firing 38-millimetre steel loops into the walls of my house – perchoom, perchoom, perchoom – made me feel like a warrior.

Growing up, I was always 'one of the boys' and that felt like a good thing. I didn't know anything about the patriarchy then, the valuing of males and masculine ways over females and feminine ones in our culture and so many others, but being admitted to the inner sanctum of maleness, listening to boys' secrets and learning to speak their language, no other girls allowed, made me feel special. I wasn't in any doubt about my own gender – I played with dolls and had roller skates and occasionally wore a dress – but none of the girls I knew wanted to goof around on skateboards or climb trees or race along bush tracks on bikes, risking bruises or a chipped front tooth (I did chip a front tooth, when I ran into a head-high gate on my way home from school one afternoon). I liked feeling as if I had a band of brothers looking out for me, and being with boys felt simpler, somehow, than being with my own kind.

One blazing January day on our annual family camping trip up the coast from Sydney, I found myself sitting on the beach in front of our campervan with some girls who also holidayed there. We were all about fifteen, but they were all curves, eyelashes and attitude; I was skinny, flat-chested and clueless. I didn't even smoke. The conversation was like a game of pass-the-parcel I couldn't keep up with. Then I noticed my brother and a few of the boys we knew learning how to windsurf, just up the beach. I made some excuse to the girls and ran over to join the boys.

'Can I have a go?' I said to an older boy dragging a windsurfer to the water's edge.

'Sure,' he said, showing me how to stand on the board and haul the sail out of the water. I only sailed a few metres before I lost my balance – and my bikini top, which was temporarily mortifying – but within a week I was skimming across the bay with my new boy-friends. Out there, my hands gripping the boom, my eyes watching for gusts, I didn't feel self-conscious or wrong; I knew how to be, without even trying.

There were days on the build that made me feel like that again, and putting up the bracing ply was one of them. George would cut each plywood sheet to the right size, Max would dab Sikaflex onto the studs and blocks, then, while they held the plywood in place, I stapled it to the studs, making little metallic stitches along the edges of each sheet. I loved the simple, physical doing-ness of it.

And, sheet by sheet, the tiny transformed from a skeletal blue-boned creature into a four-walled cocoon made of ply.

When I finished stapling the last piece of plywood into place, I lowered my staple gun to let it rest by my side and took a moment to look around from my vantage point at the top of our longest extension ladder. I was eye-to-eye with the lorikeets in the trees around us. I could smell the salt in the sea breeze up there and hear the faint rumble of the surf. I wondered what it would be like to sleep at that height.

A week later, I found out.

It was a chilly October evening. That afternoon, Max and I had dragged a foam mattress, a duvet and a couple of pillows up the builder's ladder to my sleeping loft, laid them on a makeshift plywood floor and made ourselves a bed, complete with mosquito net (tied to one of the rafters). Later, over dinner at his place, we talked easily about the design for my day loft, the kind of ladder we might make and whether my wool rug would fit up there. When bedtime came, we even held hands as we walked along the garden path by the light of the moon from his house to the tiny.

Inside, we climbed the aluminium ladder to our netted love-nest, whispering excitedly to each other like a couple of kids entering a secret clubhouse. Then, in darkness, we lay on our backs looking out the window holes at the starry sky, watching the tops of the trees dancing in a northerly gale we could actually feel on our faces as it blew through the little plywood house.

I was too excited to sleep. Instead, I listened to Max's breathing slow and become quiet; when we'd first started sharing a bed I was amazed at how silently he slept, how still he became. Never snored, rarely moved. It was unnerving, but I grew to love that sense of animal safety and contentment I felt lying next to him. I felt it envelop me in the loft that night too, my excitement easing into...

...the sound of kookaburras cackling their morning song from somewhere nearby, their voices so clear through the glassless windows.

We'd unconsciously passed another milestone: first sleep in the tiny. Followed by that dreamy newborn feeling of waking up, remembering where you are and watching someone you love do the same.

'I still can't quite believe we're doing this,' I said, propping myself up on my elbows and surveying the building site around us, below us. It was chaos, but there was so much light, so much green filling every window. From our bed, I could see the roof of Max's house, about 10 metres away, but not the road out the front or any of the neighbours' houses. My little house was in the middle of a driveway in a suburban street, and completely private.

The sun's first rays started to wink through the high eastern windows as Max sat up. 'I'm really impressed at your tenacity, Loui, and I really hope this place is all you've wanted it to be.'

'Thanks, babe. I'll never be able to repay you, you know, for everything you're doing to make this happen.'

'I know, I don't expect you to. But it's nice to hear anyway. Thank you. And you're welcome.' It was a little joke between us. I'd teased him once for not responding whenever I thanked him. I wanted to know he'd received my appreciation; he thought it immodest to expect or even acknowledge thanks. Eventually we agreed to disagree and it became a word game we played. And with that, we shimmied under the covers again and tried to forget we had a full day's work ahead of us.

⌂

One Saturday afternoon soon after our first sleep, I handed out felt pens and crayons to a few friends at what I half-seriously called a 'blessing of the tiny'. Watching everyone arrive at what had been, a few weeks earlier, just a trailer in the driveway, seeing them negotiate the primitive 'front steps' we'd made from an oil drum and a few planks, and gingerly walk into the tiny through the doorless entrance, felt... big.

First gathering in the tiny.

On tables outside, there was tea and beer, fresh scones and cake, a cheese and spinach pie with a pastry 'TH' on top (made by my friend Carmel). Inside, a small crowd of people stood around, chatty and cheerful, ducking under the diagonal braces that still criss-crossed the interior, leaning out the window holes, looking up through the rafters at the sky and the big eucalypts. I gave imaginary tours of my new home. 'This is where my desk will be, the stairs up to the sleeping loft will start here, the kitchen bench will run under these windows...'

The afternoon sun beamed in.

When I invited everyone to write or draw on the bare bracing ply walls – an extension of my secret words under the floor we were all standing on – no one was in the least bit shy about it. Carmel wrote a Mary Oliver poem. Mark the artist zoomed out, and in again: '13.8 billion years of stars collapsing and cosmic convulsions to create this home, this breath, this moment NOW.' Katie drew hearts on some of the studs. Torsten scribbled something in German. The kids drew rainbows and volcanoes and wrote their own names.

'A place for community, friendship and independence,' wrote Susan, above where my kitchen bench would be, a wish that was already coming true.

I was on a high all afternoon, riding a wave of love and goodwill for my little house, and for me.

Unlike my underfloor writings, these words were going to be visible for a while – we were still a long way off from insulating and lining the walls – and they helped me a lot in the months that followed. I'd be feeling stirred up by a clash with Max or tying myself in knots about where all the power points should go and suddenly, on the wall in front of me, I'd see *Take your time* or *Embrace imperfection* and it was as if a friend had placed her hand on my shoulder and told me everything was going to be OK.

As the sun sank behind the trees and everyone hugged goodbye and Max wandered back to his house to make dinner, I looked around at all the words on the walls, all the 'blessings', and felt a surge of gratitude for the community this little structure had gathered around itself. It might have been just a plywood box on wheels, but it was already wrapping its arms around me, holding me steady, like a true home.

Chapter 16

# Roofing vs rain

*Most people go tiny to have less stuff.* That's what I was thinking as we approached week five of the build because I seemed to be swimming against an incoming tide of stuff and every day I bought more of it: building materials, appliances, kitchen hardware. Meanwhile, my head was overflowing with stuff of its own. New skills and words, construction schedules, emotional intangibles. And still I kept trying to pour more into it.

The only thing that kept me going was the hope that, at some point, the tide would turn and things would start getting simple again. I thought putting on the roof might bring me closer to that point. It was a small roof after all: just over 7 by 2.5 metres. And I'd decided on a simple, skillion design, a single sloping surface instead of two meeting at a peak for a gable roof. How hard could it be? But, as I was learning, a tiny house is still a house – meaning it still has to be built like a house, or rather a house that's able to withstand cyclonic forces in transit.

Putting up the rafters, the first part of making the roof, had been a fiddly process, not that you'd have guessed from the way Max and George casually sat atop the wall frames, legs dangling while they hammered and chatted, like two small boys fishing from a jetty. My job, at ground level, was easier: cleaning the sheets of corrugated steel (called 'corro' in Aussie builderspeak) that would become my roof's outer shell, and checking them for corrosion and holes. I was trying to use sustainable or second-hand materials whenever I could and we were lucky enough to score some surplus sheets from a friend's building site, which we supplemented with a few more that had been languishing in Max's garage for a while. They were all in great condition, thank goodness; I had a morbid fear of leaking roofs after that minor flooding incident in my studio.

We hadn't had any real deadlines yet, but it was late October and I really wanted to get the roof on before the summer rains started, which could happen as early as November. We'd deliberately begun the build in spring to give ourselves time to make the tiny watertight before the wet season and so far we'd had ideal building weather: clear, not too hot, no rain.

But this was the north coast, where rain can come anytime. And it did come, a few days before we got the roof on.

A booming Friday afternoon thunderstorm forced us to down tools and take shelter in the garage. My main fear was that the hardwood floor inside the tiny wouldn't handle getting wet; Max and I had spread tarps over it, but as the pitter-patter turned into a downpour, I ran over to the tiny to check they were secure, before retreating to the garage. It was an odd feeling, watching heavy rain pelt my little roofless house from all angles, seeing the bracing ply change colour from light tan to dark, soaking-wet brown. If my tiny had had windows by then, they would have rattled with every grumble of thunder.

Fifteen minutes later, the sun came out – subtropical rainstorms can be like that, torrential but short-lived – and the mopping up began. We carefully lifted the tarps; they'd done their best, but the diagonal crossbeams holding up the wall frames had made them bunch up, so parts of the floor did get wet. Still, both the floor and the bracing ply dried surprisingly quickly and I learned another lesson: rain before roofing isn't always a catastrophe.

'The radiant barrier always goes *on top* of the battens,' said George, peering at me through his thick glasses. We were about to start on the next phase of the roof when we arrived at a problem: our tiny building method diverged from the traditional building method George was used to in one important way.

Think of a roof as a layer cake. On the bottom are the rafters (which run across the roof), followed by the battens (narrow strips of timber that run lengthwise, on top of the rafters), then a radiant barrier (a thin sheet of silver-sided foam designed to reflect heat to keep the inside of your home cool on hot days) and, finally, the actual roofing material (in our case, the steel sheets).

That's how things usually go. But according to our tiny house method, the radiant barrier had to go between the rafters and the battens (that is, *under* the battens) to create an insulating air gap and minimise even further the amount of radiant heat entering the tiny through the roof.

The steady hum of anxiety I felt almost every day ramped up a notch at the prospect of another conflict with George. He was the authority on the build, being the only real builder among us. So I reverted to my default position when faced with a different point of view or a clash of opinion: doubt my own. *Was I remembering the tiny house method correctly?* I needed more information.

'Why does the radiant barrier usually go on top of the battens?' I asked George.

'It's just always done that way,' he replied, squinting at the sun, his baseball cap on backwards. 'And it's trickier if you *don't* put the battens directly onto the rafters because you can't see where you're putting your nails, or where it's safe to step when you're up there. But, you know, it's your house.'

Max, standing right beside George, kept quiet. Part of me wanted his support; another part appreciated that he was staying out of it. This was my battle, my house, my decision – or mistake – to make.

'Just give me a few minutes,' I said, my heart beating fast as I jogged back to Max's house, to my 'site office' (my laptop), to burn off some nervous energy. There, I re-read my notes about roofing construction, watched a couple of how-to videos about radiant barriers, then looked up the manufacturer's instructions online – which actually recommended laying the radiant barrier *under* the battens. That was enough to convince George. He happily agreed to build my roof the way he'd never built a roof before.

Finally – after the battens and the radiant barrier were done, after we attached the gutter, after Max cut the steel sheets to size with an angle grinder, a spark-spitting power tool way above my pay grade – it was time to put on the sheets. With George and Max on the roof, which was so narrow only two people could safely work up there at a time, we needed another pair of man-hands to pass them the steel sheets, which were too awkward and heavy for me. Max made a quick call. Ten minutes later, Rosco, a hairdresser/handyman we knew who'd been offering to help on the build, arrived on his Vespa, grinning from ear to ear and looking ready for anything in his high-vis workshirt. We were good to go.

At ground level, I prepped each steel sheet by filing its cut edges and crimping the 'valleys' at each end – to stop rain from sneaking underneath and into my ceiling – before handing it to Rosco so he could carry it up a ladder and pass it to Max and George on the roof.

A couple of hours later, while Max was screwing down the very last sheet, at the rear of the tiny, I climbed a nearby tree for a magpie's view of my new roof. It suddenly looked simple again: ten and a half white steel sheets neatly lined up, side by side, sloping gently down to a single strip of guttering running along the low side. Getting the roof on is a big milestone on any build – it marks the moment when a structure becomes a shelter – so, once everyone was down off the ladders and the roof, we celebrated under the blackbean tree again, with chilled bottles of kombucha this time and little squares of the chocolate fudge I was now making every week as an on-site snack.

At the end of that week, the tiny changed outfits again when we encased it in bright-blue 'housewrap', a breathable membrane that stops moisture from building up inside the walls. As we unrolled the blue sheeting and fixed it to the bracing ply with spiky tacks we called 'ninja stars', it felt like we were creating our very own, very small art installation in the style of Christo and Jeanne-Claude, environmental artists best known for wrapping landmarks like the Arc de Triomphe in Paris, in fabric.

Max and I worked until dark that day, eager to finish the house-wrapping before another big storm that was forecast to hit later that night. We were almost done when he moved the extension ladder I was standing at the very top of, just a fraction, but without warning. I'm usually good with heights, but I felt nervous hammering in ninja stars so far off the ground, with nothing to hold onto now that the timber frame and all the window holes were entirely covered.

'Hey! Don't move my ladder without telling me, not even a little bit,' I said. Simple, direct, a clear request. I didn't usually speak to him like this, but it felt... empowering.

'Sorry,' he said, when I climbed down a few minutes later.

'That's OK, babe.'

'We're getting better at this,' he said. He slotted his hammer into a loop on his toolbelt and we hugged, before I went back to my place for the evening; being 'just friends' seemed to be working, for now.

That night, heavy rain lashed the windows and walls of my studio. By morning, water was trickling down the bedroom walls again. I couldn't wait to move out of there. And I wondered how the tiny – and its new roof – had handled the deluge. Ping. Right on cue, a message from Max: 'Tiny is high and dry.' I was beyond relieved. My little house had lived up to its latest look: as a big blue barge ready for a biblical flood.

Chapter 17

# Windows and burritos

I didn't feel as excited about the windows as I had about other parts of the build. They were beautiful objects in themselves – and more exquisitely complex than I'd expected them to be. But the daydreamer in me resented the fact that each one enclosed, a little more, the open-to-the-breeze treehouse my tiny had become. There was still plenty of light, and green views, now framed in black, but the tiny suddenly felt more closed in. More house-like, and less like a cabin in the woods.

My ambivalence about the windows also had an emotional dimension. After doing most of the roof, George and Max installed all the windows too. It wasn't an especially technical job; I could have taken Max's place, held up each window while George made sure it was level and nailed it in place. But I knew that having George's help, to make sure these first critical stages were done properly, meant letting them work together. Still, I felt excluded from this major step. It was hard, too, to see Max being so open and friendly to someone else.

'You ask too many questions,' Max said one morning that week, when I offered to help him with something. 'It's better when George and I can just focus on what we're doing.'

I hated that asking questions, something I was good at, had become a bad thing, despite me now keeping my curiosity on a short leash. But this wasn't about me, I was realising. This was Max's way of saying, 'back off'.

Just before lunch, our friend Dennis, another former Californian like George, called in. 'Hi guys!' he said, cheery as always. He commended us on our progress since his last visit before opening the bag he was carrying.

'I've got surprises!' He pulled out two burritos he'd made – for Max and George.

'Sorry, Lou,' he said, looking sheepish, 'I didn't know you'd be here.'

I wasn't angry. He'd known Max and George a long time, much longer than he'd known me, and he'd probably visited them on other building sites over the years. But it was another knock. Like in sailing when the wind changes, not in your favour, forcing you to change course. I tried to think of Dennis' comment like that, as nothing personal, just something I had to respond to, by correcting my course. So when he left and Max and George tucked into their burritos in the garage, I walked up to the house and made myself a sandwich and ate alone, wanting to be alone, to wrangle my feelings, which had their own way of seeing things.

Staying out of Max and George's way had unexpected benefits. I might not have been doing the build solo, but almost everything I did, from ordering materials and making decisions to choosing light fittings and working on-site, I was doing alone. And that actually felt OK. In one sense, it felt completely natural, figuring out this new situation for myself, finding my own way through the labyrinth of things I was learning. And the more I accepted my role as outsider, the more I relaxed.

I also started keeping my phone in the pocket of my shorts or overalls, ready to catch any incidental moments of beauty that caught my eye, the way I would snap pictures when I travelled.

That's how my photographic record of the build became punctuated with unlikely still lifes. Two M8 Nylock bolts, a couple of nuts, a bent nail and a eucalyptus flower that just happened to fall through the open roof and arrange themselves on the plywood floor (before we'd put the roof on). Ringlets of pine I'd shaved off a piece of timber with a hand-plane. Miniature metallic sculptures that littered the floor of the garage after Max spent a morning on the angle grinder trimming sheets of roofing steel. Fallen macaranga leaves, large as dinner plates, lying next to the trailer among woody blackbean seed pods. Even a small rainbow-coloured feather from one of the rowdy lorikeets that crowded the tops of the trees most afternoons as we were packing up.

Every photograph was a sea anchor that kept me from being sucked into the whirlpool of all that I was doing and feeling, all that was going on around me. I could stand in the centre of it all, observing and experiencing, and remembering that even on the hard days this was exactly where I wanted to be.

Chapter 18

# Building as therapy

Every travel writer lives a double life. There's the life we write about, which can be quite surreal and, at times, absurdly luxurious. I once stayed in a maharajah's palace that had been converted into a luxury hotel in Rajasthan and felt so overwhelmed by its opulence – and the tiger-skin floor rugs, the elephant's foot stools, the deer heads murderously mounted on the walls – I fled to the hotel's enormous pool one afternoon, only to be pursued at a respectful distance by my butler, dressed all in white but for his orange turban, who proceeded to walk up and down poolside, ready to offer me a chilled bottle of water from the silver tray he was carrying, if only I would stop swimming.

Then there's the other life, the life nobody reads about, or would want to. The one in which you're sitting at your desk, trying to write five feature stories in three days before you pack your bags and fill your head with a new destination, and deciding whether to have pasta or two-minute noodles for dinner again.

But each of these two lives needed the other. My travelling life enabled me to write, which enabled me to travel. And I loved them both. I loved being out in the world, immersing myself in a completely new place. And I loved the quiet aloneness of my home life after the busyness, the always-on-ness and the constant socialising of being away.

When the pandemic hit, I wondered how being at home all the time would affect me. So many parts of me, so many of my life skills, were related to travel and would lie dormant when I wasn't away. Much as I craved stability, I wasn't sure I was cut out for being in one place all the time.

This might have been why, as the build gathered momentum, I started to think of it as a long trip – to a place I'd never visited but had heard other people talk about. I didn't have a map, didn't speak the language, didn't know the local customs. Without even realising it, I began to do what I've always done to steady myself when I travel: I took notes. Every night, before I fell sleep, I wrote down what we'd done that day and how we did it. It was more like a ship's log than a journal, a record of random details of no interest to anyone but me, like the weight of various materials we used and lists of things I'd learned or noticed, but this nightly ritual felt as natural to me as breathing.

While the world I knew well, the one with airports and hotel rooms and itineraries and guidebooks, receded from view, occasionally shimmering like a mirage in the distance – *did I really go to all those places and do all those things?* – a new world appeared before me.

It was as fascinating to me as any new destination. *What's that called? What does this do? Why do you need one of those?* I picked up strange new words like 'brad', 'gangnail plate' and 'hoop iron' (and slang like 'fairy's fart'). I started to think in millimetres. When I ordered the joists for my two lofts from a local steel manufacturer – 'I need nine 2.4-metre lengths of 75 by 50 millimetre box section, 1.6 millimetres thick, please' – I was surprised at the sure-footedness in my voice, despite having never before said such a thing.

By the end of our second month, as I was settling into this new world,

I realised that the build was giving me a new kind of double life. For alongside my growing sadness about Max and me, something wonderful was happening.

I noticed the physical changes first. My body was becoming stronger. My hands felt the way they would feel on extended camping and hiking trips when they were called upon to do real things, in the natural world, for days or weeks on end. My arms were stronger in new ways, not from swimming or paddling a surfboard, but from carrying lengths of wood and lifting sheets of steel and using heavy power tools. Because I wasn't spending my days hunched over a keyboard staring at a computer screen, my neck wasn't aching, as it usually did. And my back felt better than it ever had, because I was constantly in motion on a build site that resembled an obstacle course; all day, every day, I was climbing up and down ladders, reaching above my head with a hammer or an impact driver in my hand, clambering onto and jumping down from the trailer.

I'd been worried the stress of the build might overwhelm me, but I felt happier and more solid in myself than I'd felt in a long time.

For all its challenges, building was its own kind of therapy, forcing me to work outside every day, in the fresh air, with other people – not indoors, at a desk, alone. Having to concentrate on what I was doing, particularly because I was doing so many things for the first time, meant there was less time for rumination. There were tangible signs of progress – and little dopamine hits of accomplishment – as my little house took shape. And just working towards a goal, no matter how long it was going to take to reach it or how meandering the trail that led to it, was supremely grounding, particularly with the pandemic creeping closer to us with every news bulletin.

Because we were building in Max's driveway, and could be seen from the road, we often had visitors. People we knew, and others just interested to know what we were doing, would see us working and drop in. I didn't like surprise visits when I was writing; the right words could too easily be spooked by other people or loud noises. But on the build, a visit was a chance to take a break and, because people almost always wanted to see inside the tiny-in-progress, a reminder of what we were doing and why we were doing it.

Whenever someone stepped into the tiny for the first time, even at this early stage, I'd see their face change. It wasn't just surprise that so much could fit into such a small space. It was something that small dwellings often bring out in people, I've noticed: a sense of play and possibility. I could almost hear them thinking: *Why* not *sleep in a loft and have a ladder inside your house?* And: *Could I live in a place like this?*

I gave impromptu tours, which felt slightly exposing sometimes. Showing someone you don't know around the house you've designed to snugly fit your life, your habits, your body... It's like standing naked in front of a stranger. After all those years of renting, dodging others' opinions and judgements – this was the landlord's choice of wall colour, that was my flatmate's couch – I had to stand by my decisions. And embrace my domestic vanity; I wanted people to like both me and my little house.

We had a few non-human visitors, too. One morning a grasshopper hitched a ride on a ladder I was carrying. Spiders colonised undisturbed corners inside. After a sprinkling of rain, we found a bright green tree frog in a puddle on the tarp protecting the floor. A few weeks later, butcherbirds perched on my new roof, making the most of this new vantage point in their territory, and a magpie began visiting, strutting around the sawhorses and hopping up on workbenches in the garage like a small feathered foreman. Outside, moths hid in plain sight, camouflaged on stacks of cedar weatherboards we were about to use for the cladding. All around my little house, there was life, embracing this new addition to the neighbourhood.

Chapter 19

# The rough and the smooth

'So, which side are we going to have facing out?' It was early November and I was excited about the tiny's next costume change: from being wrapped in blue to being clad in western red cedar and grey steel. 'The rough side or the smooth side? I like the look of the smooth side.' I ran my hands along one of the honey-coloured cedar weatherboards, which had a different texture on each side, and I wanted to make sure Max, George and I were on the same page before we started nailing them in place.

'We've already talked about this, several times,' George said, impatience nibbling at his words. 'The *rough* side always goes out.' A pause. 'But I'll do whatever you want.'

He had told me that a few weeks earlier, when a truckload of cedar was delivered. I hadn't forgotten. But since then I'd come to prefer the smooth side – it was less 'hairy' than the rough side – and I wondered if there was a practical reason we couldn't put that side out instead. *Was the rough side more waterproof? Or was it just 'always done that way'?* I wanted to understand, and discussion helped me make decisions. Instead, I'd been put in my place.

Leaving George's words hanging in the air, I retreated to a shady spot out of sight of the tiny, where I sat on a rock, poured myself a glass of water and exhaled. I needed time to think.

'Hello!' It was Katie, who lived in the small apartment attached to Max's house. On her way to work, she was friendliness personified, like sunshine after a wet week. 'How are things going today?'

'Hey,' I said, basking in her sunshine. 'They're going, um, OK.' A couple of tears sneaked past my façade.

She sat down on the rock beside me. 'What's going on?'

It wasn't about the cedar. Or George. 'It's just a bit grim at the moment between Max and me,' I said. 'Just feeling a bit... alone.'

'That's understandable.' She really did seem to understand, which suddenly made me feel less alone and reminded me that there were moments of friendliness and simple connection everywhere, often where I least expected to find them. When I called the 'special orders' number at the hardware store, for instance, and heard the receptionist's sing-song voice say, 'Hello, Bunnings Hardware, this is Shaz!' When I spoke to suppliers and they instantly understood what I said, the first time I said it. When someone on the beach or in the supermarket returned my 'Good morning' smile. And just seeing Katie coming and going each day was a good thing. I had to get more women on-site, I decided.

Nothing more was said about rough sides or smooth sides, but cladding the main wall was a three-person job; because the weatherboards were so long, it took three of us to hold and nail each one in place. George even made three identical 'jigs' from scraps of pine, one for each of us, with our initials scrawled on them, which we used to check that each board went up level and overlapped the one below it by exactly the same amount, all the way along its length. (In woodworking, a jig helps you guide or position pieces of wood while you work on them.)

One by one, with pauses to trim some of the boards to fit around the windows, the cedar crept up the wall and my little blue house started to look like a cabin again.

The next day, with most of the eastern wall done, I remarked to no one in particular how smooth the cedar looked, smoother than expected – considering we'd put the rough side facing out, because it always goes out.

George looked at me oddly. 'Well, that *is* the smooth side. Because that's what you wanted.'

It took me a moment to understand. He'd yielded to *my* wishes? I felt foolish for not noticing until then, but there was a lot of variation between the boards; the 'smooth' side often looked rough, and vice versa. And I was still a rookie. What I didn't understand was: why hadn't George (or Max) said anything? *What was going on, what was I missing?* I've had easier interactions with people when we haven't shared a common language. Maybe that was it: I had to learn to speak George.

Although we'd started cladding as a team of three, we soon reached a height where George and Max had to carry on without me. Partly because there was space for only two of us to stand on the painters' plank (a narrow aluminium platform supported by an A-frame ladder at each end), which they were using to clad the high sections of the wall we couldn't reach from the ground. And partly because, as Max told me, he and George were worried about my 'safety on the ladders', which seemed absurd. I'd been climbing up and down ladders without problems for two months. I was more agile, and ten years younger, than George. But I didn't argue. I let them work the way they wanted to, with the cedar and with the steel cladding after that, another two-person job.

A build is never as singular as it sounds; it's made up of thousands of pieces that all need to be coordinated and choreographed. So while Max and George continued with the cladding, I turned my attention to the interior. I redrew the plans for my stairs, had a long conversation about kitchens with a design consultant, finished making the plywood floors for my two lofts – and kept ducking outside to see what was happening on the other side of the walls, which was: board by cedar weatherboard, sheet by steel sheet, the cladding encircled the tiny.

As Max and George wrestled the last sheet into place, I finished oiling a small stack of 'shiplap' planks of western red cedar we were going to use on the front of the tiny, a simple job that made me inexplicably happy. I was in love with this wood: the feel of it under my fingers, its lightness (one of the reasons I'd chosen it), its sauna-like smell. With every brushstroke of oil, the cedar came alive in caramel swirls, brooding chocolates and wave-like contour lines. It had come from big evergreen trees in North America, Australia's own stands of red cedar having been logged to near-extinction long ago, but the colour of it – alongside with the dark grey steel – seemed perfectly at home in this part of the world.

They were the colours of this country, I realised that afternoon when I took a break to drink some water; outside the tiny, I leaned against a retaining wall made of basalt boulders topped with small logs from eucalypts trimmed on-site by a professional tree-lopper before we'd started the build. They were the colours I saw every day in nature: dark volcanic rock, honeyed native timber. No wonder they looked so right together, so right for this place.

⌂

On the drive to our next couples' session, Max and I chatted amiably about everything except us. But as soon as we took our seats in Sean's office, two weeks of hurt and frustration bubbled to the surface. Max's voice stayed calm, keeping a lid on his feelings, while I felt increasingly distressed and far from everything good in my life and all the peace I'd felt lately. Instead I saw myself through Max's eyes, as an unpredictable bundle of anxiety, insecurities and too much emotion.

Sean listened to us both.

Then Max announced that this would be his last session. A unilateral decision that would affect us both. He'd got all he needed from the sessions, he said. As if our issues had nothing to do with him.

I wanted to be angry, but, on an impulse, I reached my hand towards him, rested it on the side of his chair. Without hesitation he took my hand in both of his, held onto it tightly as if he were holding onto me, and us.

Outside, after the session, Max and I hugged, and relief mingled with unease. I knew what we had wasn't healthy, and that things weren't changing, but it felt good to reconnect, and the love was still there, so strongly that a moment like this could reel me back in. That night, we talked while he made us dinner at his place. He was present and friendly. There was no attitude or defensiveness. My heart fell open.

We cuddled sleepily at first light the next morning, then drove to the beach for a swim. As if nothing had ever been wrong between us and never would be again.

And as the cladding crept up the walls that month, the love crept back into our relationship. We started surfing together again, swam in the sea together, sang together and had date nights again and sleepovers. There were sneaky skinny dips in the lake. Breakfasts in the sun on his daybed. Sunday afternoons in a hammock in the shade of the paperbarks.

We even worked together without any upsets or misunderstandings. It was delightful, and disorienting. *What was happening?* Just as I was beginning to let go of him, he was showing me what I would be letting go of, a future full of moments like these.

Chapter 20

# 'Lace petticoat' work

One of my earliest memories is of sitting naked at Mum's sewing machine, aged three, legs swinging, pretending to sew. I wanted to do what Mum did. Before she married Dad, she'd been a portrait photographer by trade, but she was a fashion designer by nature and she *loved* making clothes. Whenever she and Dad went to a dinner party or to some gala event (Dad worked in advertising), Mum would emerge from their bedroom looking fabulous in one of her own creations: a silk pantsuit, a sequinned evening dress, a backless summer frock. Actually she always looked stylish, even if she was just popping to the shops. One of our neighbours called her 'the fast-moving mannequin'.

When I was old enough, Mum tried to pass on to me her love of haute couture. It was no use. I got bored watching her cut fabric and grumped about having to stand still in my underwear while she pinned a new garment to my fidgety frame. But I liked sitting with her at the dining table, the latest fashion magazines fanned out before us, talking about the pictures and plucking ideas from the glossy pages. And I loved the things she made for me: sundresses and bikinis, jumpsuits (Mum would have loved that these are back in fashion), even slinky cocktail dresses that made me feel like a mermaid.

She made me a corporate skirt-suit once, too, for my first real job, from fine black wool, the kind usually reserved for men's suits. It had a short, fitted jacket and a slim, knee-length skirt lined with slippery black satin and Mum had hemmed the satin lining with a strip of black lace only I would see, a nod to the art of making something beautiful for its own sake.

When she died and I started travelling and no longer needed clothes that required ironing or dry cleaning, I reluctantly gave away that skirt-suit and forgot all about Mum's act of practical love – until three months into the build.

It was early December and the cladding was done, the windows were in, the roof was on. We were entering the undramatic belly of the build, the progress we were making less visible than it had been. But before we could start assembling the interior – the kitchen cabinets, the timber bench top, the plywood walls and ceiling – we had to put a few finishing touches to the exterior. That included tidying up a few things on the tiny that weren't essential to its structural integrity, things only Max and I would ever know about and no one would ever see – unless they crawled under the tiny or climbed onto its roof.

I called it 'lace petticoat' work, for Mum. I might have been a terrible student when she tried to teach me to sew, but I did learn something from her, from the way she lived and worked: the importance of doing whatever you're doing as well as you can, and with love. Which meant, to me, taking care with small, insignificant tasks as well as big, important ones.

I thought about this a lot while I did my 'lace petticoat' jobs that week. With the smallest paintbrush I could find in the hardware store, I touched up small scratches on the fascia boards just below the guttering, way too high to see from ground level. I painted bits of bracing ply partially hidden by flashing. I dabbed dark-grey paint on four screws under the doorstep, which would be completely concealed once we'd built the deck. I trimmed ragged bits of housewrap that peeked out (if you'd have been looking) from under the bottom edge of the cladding.

It was one of the quietest and most satisfying parts of the build, each unremarkable task connecting me to my little house in subtle, hard-to-reach ways that more momentous jobs hadn't, just as Mum had taught me.

Chapter 21

# How not to build a wall

By mid-December, the tiny was looking good, on the outside. Inside, it was an empty box, all sawdust, exposed studs and sheets of thick black plastic protecting the hardwood floor. Having helped us get this far, George took a break. I was excited, and a little nervous, about working with Max, just the two of us. At least the next job on our list was a simple one, which I wanted to tackle, under Max's supervision: to build an internal stud wall, the only one in the tiny, which would separate the bathroom and the kitchen.

But the afternoon we planned to start the wall, I was in a funk. The night before I'd had an uncomfortable phone call with my brother, Tim, who lived in Sydney. We usually got along well, but he'd been critical, in that phone call, of all the work Max and I had done, despite never having built anything himself. I'd explained that we had everything under control, and experienced friends like George helping us. He hadn't listened, and instead of letting it roll over me, laughing it off or remembering that Tim always had his own perspective on things (as a boy, he often had passionate disagreements with our encyclopedias), I let his words stick to my insides. I'd really wanted his support.

'I can't do it,' I told Max when he started getting out the tools I would need.

'You know you can,' he said.

'Any other day maybe,' I said, taking off my toolbelt. 'But I'm feeling so flat. I think I just need to go home.'

Maybe it was the chance to finally work with Max that kept me there or the fact that he was on my side again, but I decided to do the wall. Or at least make a start on it.

Something I love about carpentry: at its most elemental, it's about attaching bits of wood to each other. I reminded myself of this as I measured and cut and nailed together various lengths of pine that would form the uprights and the horizontal blocks of my wall. The summer sun beamed into the garage and I got lost in the doing, began to climb out of my slump.

Max hovered nearby as I worked, peppering me with tips that were helpful but relentless: hold the hammer like this, put your feet there, the wood should be at this angle. At one point, he tried to take the hammer out of my hand to show me something, just as he'd done when we'd worked on those chairs before the build; I didn't let him take it, told him I'd figure it out for myself, thanks anyway. He backed off – until I needed his help again. This was our see-saw of power. I wanted his help, but not the attitude that came with it, which fed my own self-doubting thoughts, which weren't entirely unwarranted.

Just a few weeks earlier I'd made a classic rookie mistake. I'd had to move the registration plate on the rear bumper of the trailer to make way for the cladding. A quick job: take out the two screws holding the plate in place, drill two new holes, re-insert the screws in their new positions. Things were going well until I got to the second screw. I couldn't get the drill bit to make a new hole. *Was the drill bit blunt?* I leaned into the hilt of the drill, the way Sophie had shown me. *What was*

*I doing wrong?* I finally called Max over.

'Show me what you're doing,' he said.

I pressed the drill bit to the steel bumper again and squeezed the trigger. The drill bit was spinning, no hole was being made.

'Did you put the drill in reverse?' he said.

'Yeah, to remove that screw I just took out,' I said, instantly realising my mistake. 'Oh, man!' I'd been trying to drill into galvanised steel with my drill *in reverse*! 'You're never going to let me forget this are you?' I laughed.

'Wait 'til I tell Georgie! Happens to the best of us, bub,' he said, laughing too.

Making the wall in the garage that afternoon, I wasn't feeling so cocky. The soft part of me still wanted to go home. The air was hot and still. Mosquitoes buzzed around us. Sweat dripped down my face, down my back, soaked my bra. I was so tired. But I couldn't leave. I had to keep going. This wasn't the way I'd imagined us building together. This felt like a test I had to pass.

It was almost dark when I nailed the last two pieces of pine together. Still feeling flushed from the heat and utterly exhausted, I put my hammer down and stood back to admire my handiwork. I'd made a wall. A small one, barely bigger than a door, but a timber-framed wall, fair and square. I carried it into the tiny and slotted it into place. A perfect fit. I thanked Max for his help, gave him a hug and drove home feeling victorious, and defeated.

It wasn't just that I'd forced myself to keep going when I'd felt like giving up. It was that I'd somehow abandoned myself in the process, when Max had turned his lighthouse love on me. I'd slipstreamed off his energy and belief in me. So when I reached the end, I wasn't fully there.

I lay on the concrete floor at my place and waited for myself to catch up. *Why did I keep doing this?* I could have steered myself into calmer waters. Instead I'd silenced my own internal compass. I'd got lost again. This wasn't just about Max and me, this was about my own relationship with me, about how I wanted to build my home, how I wanted to be in the world, a reminder that sometimes the *how* is more important than the *what* or even the *why*.

Chapter 22

# Dear anxiety

I don't remember being an anxious child, but something happened when I was about seven that implanted an invisible, striving nervousness that could wander into my life uninvited and sometimes stay awhile.

I was playing in the front yard of our house with my best friend, Jenny, wearing a lime-green sundress Mum had made, feeling happy. It must have been early spring because of what we were doing: picking velvety buds from a peach tree and 'putting them to bed' under blankets of moss at the base of the tree, like small faceless dolls without arms or legs. It sounds creepy now, not to mention destructive, but we were completely entranced by this activity we'd invented. So I didn't notice Dad's car pulling into the driveway, didn't hear him walking up the sandstone path, didn't hear him clearing his throat, until his trouser legs and leather shoes were right beside me.

I was kneeling on the soft moss, tucking in another peach bud.

'What the hell are you doing?!' I looked up, wide-eyed, at Dad's face, which had become puffy and red. I remember feeling afraid, then sorry for him. *Daddy's angry. I've made Daddy angry.* It was the 1970s and smacking was still a thing, but I don't remember him unbuckling his belt that day. The sudden reversal from having fun to having done something wrong packed enough of an emotional punch to hardwire my young brain. I guess that's where it started, a sense of foreboding that, any moment now, someone was going to tap me on the shoulder and tell me I was doing something wrong or in the wrong way or had forgotten something important (such as, peach buds grow into peaches and, eventually, new peach trees).

Is it possible to inherit anxiety? Does it sometimes soak into us from the waters we swim in, in our families and our wider surroundings, as we grow up? I think at least some of Dad's anger, then and at other times, was just anxiety that was afraid of itself, afraid to be seen. Maybe that's how I learned that anxiety was something you shouldn't show others. But when I think about that spring day now, there's no emotional charge in it. I just see a little girl distracted by play and her love of small things momentarily losing sight of the big picture (which still happens to me sometimes), and her father simply not knowing what to do with that.

If I learned from Mum the joy of making something beautiful, I learned from Dad to find the mistakes you're also making along the way and to correct them, before anyone else can catch you out. Twin forces in my life that took turns at the wheel. But, to be honest, Dad's way, and the fear underneath it, probably took hold of me more often, made me want to do things well, at first to please him, then to appease my own inner critic.

I'd got into the habit of watching the shimmy of anxious, self-critical thoughts at meditation retreats I used to do, years ago. Sitting on my cushion, these thoughts would come, say their piece and disappear again, like actors on a stage. Watching them robbed them of their power, helped me see them as just shadow-puppets on the wall, but they never completely disappeared. I just got used to them humming under the surface of other, more useful or more pleasant thoughts, sometimes softly, sometimes – on a deadline, during an argument, when the stakes were high, when I was in a rush – more loudly, when they'd scream through my brain and seize control of my body.

On the build they could scream. So I listened to the anxiety as I worked, watched when it would peak (when starting a new task) and when it would quieten down (when I got the hang of what I was doing) and tried to accept it, even welcome it. All emotions are messengers, Sean had said once; they're just trying to tell us something, give us information we can use to take care ourselves and others.

Being near Max ramped up the anxiety, too, because things were always unpredictable when we were together. So I paid close attention to the ebb and flow of my emotions around him, and devised a strategy whenever I needed his help: ask for instruction, then work alone. Without Max watching me, I could concentrate more easily on what I needed to do and figure out my own way of doing it. When I did that, I could even enjoy what I was doing and forget all about myself – and the anxiety. Until the next new task came along.

I started to notice gender differences on our build site, too. Max and I would often clash when we had to physically do something together, like carry a long piece of timber from one place to another. He would pick up one end, tell me to grab the other and start walking. If I asked where we were going – just so I'd know if I needed to get a firmer grip or put on my gloves – he'd get annoyed. *Don't make the men angry.*

Then Sean gave me a helpful tip; I'd started seeing him for individual sessions after Max had dropped out of couples' therapy.

'You probably know this already,' he told me one day, 'but guys often like to figure things out *while* they're doing something, using spatial and visceral clues, whereas women often like to know what they're doing *before* they start doing it.'

Yes! I'd seen this before, when I'd taught kids how to surf: the boys would usually run straight to the water with their surfboards, to learn by doing, while the girls wanted to know what they were going to do, and why, before they paddled out.

I found it a lot easier to work with Max after that: instead of asking questions, I'd do as he asked, figure it out as we did it, as he did. Peace was restored, in those situations at least. The feminist in me squirmed. *Why is it so often the* woman *who has to understand and adapt while the man sails on, oblivious, doing what he's always done, the way he's always done it?* Until I reminded myself Max was helping me to build my house. Besides, I figured anything that minimised conflict between us was a good thing. And although I really didn't need anything else to think about, I found it kind of fascinating, this live, interactive experiment in human relations going on right in front of me.

## Chapter 23

# String work

The week before Christmas, a Thursday morning, my friend Susan offered to help me with the next task: attaching lengths of string to all the rafters to hold my wool insulation batts in place and stop them falling on our heads when we started putting up the ceiling. A few days earlier, Max had suggested I drill holes through all the rafters, four or five in each, to thread the string through; this would leave a clear surface for us to attach the plywood ceiling to, under the rafters. It sounded like a good idea; I agreed to do that.

It was a steamy day, the air thick from all the recent rain. When Susan arrived at the tiny, George and Max were already working in one of the lofts, putting extra blocks in the stud walls in preparation for putting up the plywood walls. I'd just started explaining to her what we were going to do with the string when George, who'd overheard me, peeked over the edge of the loft.

'That's going to take *forever*!' he said. 'It'll be quicker if you just run the pieces of string along underneath each rafter and fix them in place with some small, U-shaped nails.'

Max and I had ruled out this option because we'd thought the string and the nails would make the plywood ceiling bulge where it touched the

Our first big milestone: putting up the timber frame

George and I marking-up the bottom plate in preparation for making the frame

The 'plywood box' phase of my tiny's development

Cross-bracing inside the tiny to give extra support to the walls until the roof went on

Stapling the bracing ply to the timber frame was suprisingly empowering

Max and George putting on the last of the recycled roofing sheets

One of the many 'blessings' written by friends on the bracing ply walls

Beauty on the build: two M8 Nylock bolts, a bent nail and some eucalyptus flowers

Making my first ever internal wall frame taught me an important lesson

Plank by plank, the cedar cladding crept up the walls, progressively hiding the tiny's undershirt of bright-blue housewrap

The tiny as a treehouse-cabin (above) before the windows; and the lake where I swam

Max and George working on the beautiful shiplap cedar cladding at the front of the tiny

Working on the interior meant learning to live with chaos – and a snowstorm of insulation batts

The niche above the timber bench became a place for natural treasures

A stone love-letter Max gave me, halfway through the build

The long timber bench (right) with its 'live edge' and rustic butterfly joints

One of three flowers I made from leftover pieces of cedar cladding

Using the dropsaw to cut the architraves to size

The 'I finally have a front door!' milestone

Even after months of building, making these four cedar buttons quietly blew my mind

The finished interior, looking towards my desk, couch and day loft (up the ladder)

One of my favourite features was outside: my outdoor shower

The view from my day loft, looking down to the kitchen and across at the birch-ply stairs leading to the bed loft

The finished exterior (above and below); sitting outside with a cup of tea (right), looking up at the giant eucalypts towering above

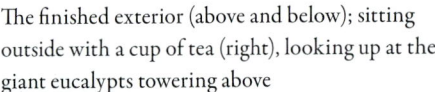

rafters, but George insisted it'd be fine. I had to make a snap decision; Susan could only spare a couple of hours and I had to get the strings done before I drove to the Gold Coast to visit Dad that afternoon, so that Max and George could start putting up the ceiling while I was away.

I decided to take George's advice. Max didn't say anything, so I assumed he was OK with the change of plan. *Maybe he'll be pleased*, I thought, *that I'd listened to George, been flexible and made a decision without dithering.*

Susan and I climbed a ladder into the other loft and got to work. While she fed out the string from a spool, I pinned it to the underside of the rafters by hammering in the U-shaped nails. A retired science teacher, Susan was one of the smartest people I knew, but she knew even less about building than I did. At last, I had my own apprentice! It was lovely to work with another woman, too, and a good friend; I could relax knowing that no relationship issues or power dynamics were going to make a surprise appearance.

There was a great vibe in the tiny that morning. Max and George talked happily as they worked; Susan and I did the same. I got into some awkward positions, sometimes lying on my back on the painters' plank, sometimes doing kneeling back-bends to hammer in the nails above me, which amused everyone. And we finished the job sooner than expected.

After Susan left, I drove north. It felt good to get out of town and away from the build for a couple of days, and the pandemic hadn't yet closed the NSW–Queensland border. Since moving to the north coast, I'd become a bit of a country mouse, but I liked visiting Dad; we were enjoying each other's company more than we had earlier in my life and I enjoyed the change of scene, too, particularly the high-rise views of the Gold Coast's long beaches and urban skyline from his apartment. I checked in with Max each night, asked how the ceiling was looking; his replies were cool and brief, but all seemed to be going to plan.

Returning to the tiny early on Saturday morning, I felt refreshed and excited to see my new ceiling. When we met in the driveway, Max didn't hug me hello, but I was almost used to that now. We walked into the tiny together.

The ceiling looked beautiful, all the sheets snug up against each other with *no bulges*, thank goodness. I climbed up onto a painters' plank suspended between two ladders, for a closer look, and noticed all the nails that attached the plywood sheets to the rafters; two rows of them, at every seam. They did *not* look beautiful. But Max reassured me that they weren't going to stay like that; we could make them disappear by 'punching' them deeper into the plywood with a hammer and a metal spike called a nail-punch. The holes could then be covered with wood putty and sanded smooth. This was going to be my job for the next few days: nail-punching and puttying. Every. Single. Nail. In my entire ceiling.

Then we started talking about the decision I'd made about the string, two days earlier. Everything had turned out fine, but Max seemed miffed that I'd changed my mind, abandoned his idea in favour of George's. I thought it might help to let him know I valued his opinion.

'Hey, if it comes up again that George and I have different ideas, I'd really like to know what you think.' I was trying to make it sound like what it was: a request, not a demand. I told him I still felt a bit intimidated when George challenged me. 'Maybe you could say something to back me up or remind me why we'd decided to do it another way?'

In the time it took my words to cover the short distance from where

I was sitting on the plank to where Max was standing in the doorway, their intention got lost.

He was *always* supporting me, he said, always backing me when there were differences of opinion between me and George, between our tiny house method and traditional construction. He seemed to be trying to make a point, to let something out that had been lurking for too long in the shadows. It finally came out.

'Do you want to know how I feel? You're *always* asking me how I feel,' he said, his pitch rising. 'How do I *feel*? I feel like I'm a *second-class citizen* in your life. I know sometimes you feel like that. I've heard all that. I'm telling you what *I* feel, OK? I feel like I'm the one being picked on, I'm the one who's not good enough, even though I've gone through things with you *time and time again*, it's never fucking enough. *That's* how I feel. I feel pain in here,' he thumped his chest. 'I feel loss, I feel angst, I feel hurt. Continuously I feel hurt.'

I opened my arms and he walked over to me and rested his head against my legs and I placed my hands on his head.

He looked up at me with red eyes. 'And the last thing I want to do is put more pressure on you, so I hold a lot of that in.'

'You can tell me,' I said. All I wanted was for him to tell me.

'I can't tell you a lot of the time because it bounces back,' he said.

'I know what you mean. It's the same for me...'

'I don't *care* what it is for you. I don't want to hear about you. I hear about you *all the time*.' All those times I'd thought being open and vulnerable would help us connect.

'That's not true. We haven't talked about any of this stuff lately,' I said.

'I'm not interested. I'm here. This is pain. This is suffering. This is hurt.'

I felt relieved that he'd finally told me how he'd been feeling. That he hadn't walked away this time. I let his pain in and all his words, all his hurt, and let my heart break again, for both of us, for feeling so hurt and broken and sad around each other. Everything stopped and became quiet and we held onto each other, like survivors from a shipwreck of our own making.

Late that afternoon I drove to the lake for an after-work swim with one of my travel writer friends, Angela, and her two-year-old son, Ollie. It was comforting to be around someone who'd known me before I'd met Max, to talk about trips she was planning, to remember the world beyond the driveway. And being in the water always soothed me.

After our swim we sat on the grass and while Angela and I talked, Ollie climbed onto my lap and I smoothed his wet hair and he closed his eyes and fell asleep. Just like that. The weight of his small body calmed me as much as I had apparently calmed him, which surprised me given how fractured the day had been. In the midst of everything going on, it seemed, there was still something settled and grounded inside me, holding on.

Chapter 24

# A tiny Christmas

Max's outpouring didn't change or resolve anything. We were softer with each other for a couple of days, sorrow and satisfaction in the air we breathed as we worked, but he was persistently distant and out of reach. I immersed myself in the slow, methodical job of making all the nails in the ceiling disappear, using my hammer, a nail-punch and some putty.

At the end of one workday, I turned to him as I was packing up my tools, trying to read his face, wondering if I should say something.

'It feels as if you don't really like me or want to be around me,' I said quietly. There, it was out. I felt better.

'I *don't* like you or want to be around you,' he said.

It hurt, of course it did, but at least he hadn't denied or dismissed what I'd noticed. That almost made it hurt less.

There was no time to reply, even if I had known what to say, because at that moment three of his friends, including George, strolled up the driveway carrying guitars and amps for an afternoon jam at Max's house. I waved hello to them and withdrew to the tiny where I immersed myself in another slow, methodical (but noisier) job: sanding the ceiling. Holding the orbital sander overhead was tiring and awkward. It made my neck and shoulders ache, my safety glasses kept fogging up in the humid heat and I had to sand the entire ceiling twice, with two grades of sandpaper – but I wanted it to be uncomfortable and I wanted to do something I didn't have to think about. I wanted to not think or feel anything for a while.

Max and I didn't pick up that conversation later, just added it to the pile of others like it, which we stepped around in our daily interactions with each other. But we managed to call a truce for Christmas and took the day off, had a surf together and a quiet lunch at his place. I always liked the stillness of Christmas Day, the closed shops, the quiet roads – though the pandemic was making such stillness more common now. The peace of the day seeped into us.

Then we got back to work.

Boxing Day was, for us, Bathroom Day. It was just Max and me and we were communicating well enough again to work side by side. While he cut to size the cement sheets that would become the walls and ceiling of my bathroom (more practical than ceramic tiles when your house is mobile), I cut insulation batts, tailoring them to fit all the spaces in the walls. It was like shearing a sheep with a butterknife – dagger grip on my Stanley, sweat dripping off me, blisters on my thumb, the polyester fleece so tough I had to keep replacing the blade.

Three days later, my little bathroom was finished (except for the waterproof flooring, which would come later). But my insulation work had just begun. I had to measure, cut and stuff recycled batts into all the wall spaces in the rest of the tiny, in preparation for installing the plywood walls. After working in one of the lofts one morning – the hottest part of the tiny, at the hottest time of the day, at the hottest time of the year – I climbed down the ladder for a glass of water, feeling sweaty and rosy-cheeked from the heat, just as Max stepped inside.

'You look beautiful,' he said, suddenly seeing me again.

The first day of a new year. I'd woken up in the dark and walked barefoot to a grassy spot on the headland, close to where Max and I had had our first picnic, almost four years, and a lifetime, ago. I sat on the grass, and waited.

There. Electric-edged clouds, a subtle signpost. First sunrise of the year.

I poured myself a cup of tea from the thermos I'd brought, and opened my notebook. Stared at the sun, looked down at the page. A ritual, the first words of a new year. *What did I want to say?* I started writing down my thanks for the year just gone, for the thousand and one blessings I'd received. I took a sip of tea. And waited for something else I knew was coming, the sadness that was never far away now, under everything.

For years I'd been following a lonely road, trying not to want or need anything more, or anyone. Then I found Max and thought I'd found where I belonged, someone to belong to. But home was supposed to be a safe place, where you felt appreciated and understood, and, increasingly, I didn't feel those things. More and more, it hurt just being around him. I knew then, sitting on the grass with my tears blurring the morning sun, that if things didn't change, a hard decision was coming and might arrive sooner than I expected.

Chapter 25

# Which white did I like?

Working on the interior of the tiny turned out to be just as physical as working on its exterior – and took twice as long, which surprised me. I just figured there were two halves to a build: inside and outside. But we still had a long way to go.

After finishing the bathroom, we started on the plywood walls. Max and I worked steadily together, cutting each plywood sheet – made of falcata, a type of wood almost as lightweight as balsa – to fit its final destination in the kitchen or one of the lofts or behind the couch. It was like a jigsaw puzzle, one in which we made the pieces as we played. To do that, I learned how to use another kind of jigsaw – the power-tool kind with a vertical blade – to make holes for my windows, light fittings, switches and power points, after I'd first triple-checked that I wanted those lights, switches and power points in those exact locations.

Every day, a few more sheets went up. Sometimes we'd work until dark, slapping at the mosquitoes that savaged our arms and legs. We were making good progress. But halfway through the wall-making, Max told me he wanted to pick up the pace, was going to ask George to work with us again, for a couple of days a week. My heart sank; the interior was supposed to be our part of the build, the bit we did together. I didn't want to feel sidelined again, given small jobs while Max and George did the real work.

But when George joined us, that didn't happen. Maybe I'd changed, maybe we all had, but we each knew our place and settled into it. While Max and George wrangled the wall sheeting, I tap-tap-tapped away with my hammer, reprising the work I'd done on the ceiling to hide the nails around the edges – and down the middle – of the plywood walls. With decision fatigue setting in now that we'd been on the build for almost four months, I relished any simple, repetitive tasks I could get my hands on. The simpler and more repetitive, the better.

Some days, Max took a day off to work at George's house and I got the chance to work in the tiny alone, nail-punching or puttying or sanding smooth the nail-sized putty dots. There was less anxiety those days, just a meditative doing, at my own pace, while the tiny began to look more and more like somewhere I could live.

⌂

Once all the plywood walls were up, it was time for us to change the tiny's look yet again – by painting the walls white. But which white? I collected paint chips and charts and catalogues like a bowerbird. I scoured home renovation websites, talked to friends who were interior designers or had just painted their own houses, learned about warm whites and cool whites. The names alone seduced me: Whisper White, Cotton Sheets, Silver Feather, Snow Peak, Dogwood Blossom. They were ghostly, wintry, swan-like. There were whites for chic gallery walls and whites for sun-soaked living rooms.

It was all starting to sound like a Dr Seuss book. Which white did I like?

Eventually, I narrowed my options down to Lexicon Half and Lexicon Quarter, both unwittingly apt for a writer's home, I thought, and almost identical. I painted sample swatches on my bare plywood walls so I could see how each white looked in different light, at different times of the day, until I forgot which white was which. I was still scrolling through design websites on my phone in the Bunnings car park moments before I finally walked in and bought a 4-litre tin of Lexicon Quarter. This, I learned, was 4 litres of Dulux's standard white base paint with one drop of black paint in it. Lexicon Half apparently had *two* drops of black paint. I had spent two weeks deliberating over a single drop of paint.

After that, the painting itself was a breeze, mainly because our friend Wal, a retired housepainter, had offered to help. Softly spoken with a gentle manner, Wal was a skinny surfer in his late sixties and his painting outfit hadn't changed since about 1975: white T-shirt, short white cotton shorts and a pair of white Dunlop Volleys.

He might have been retired, but Wal was still a pro. When he turned up for his first day on the job, he brought several drop sheets and all his own brushes, scrapers and spatulas, of all sizes and shapes, in an old metal toolbox that opened like a magic trick to reveal multiple cantilevered shelves and compartments inside.

He also had a habit of repeating things he said, something I found oddly comforting.

'I reckon leave it for another couple of weeks before you put a third coat on, Lou,' Wal told me early in the build when he called in and saw me oiling the cedar cladding.

'Thanks, Wal, I will,' I replied.

He walked over to Max, who was working in the garage. 'I told

Lou, better wait two weeks before doing a third coat on that cedar,' Wal told Max.

'OK, Wal,' said Max, who had probably heard Wal telling me the same thing moments before.

Then Wal walked back to me. 'Lou, I told Max you might want to leave it for two weeks, then put a third coat on.'

'Great, thanks Wal,' I said, sneaking a glance at Max, trying not to smile.

It could go on like this for days. Before starting a job, Wal would pop in to check what needed to be done. He'd come the next day, too, just to be sure. Sometimes he'd phone between visits to tell me what he'd told me the day before. I'd listen and agree. He wasn't hard of hearing or absent-minded. It was just Wal's way – he was a perfectionist who liked to make sure everyone was on the same wavelength – and one of his most endearing qualities. We loved him. And I loved that there were never any misunderstandings or surprises when I worked with him.

One of the joys of building a tiny is that major jobs, like painting your entire house, don't take forever. Each coat of paint took Wal and me about three hours (while Max busied himself with other things) and we did four coats. Within a few days, we were done.

It helped that Wal did the trickiest, most time-consuming part: the 'cutting in'. This involves carefully painting the edges of the walls – where they meet the ceiling, the floor or the windows – without the aid of 'painter's tape' (which Wal never used) and without getting paint where it wasn't wanted. He'd paint the perimeter of each wall like this and I'd follow with a lambswool roller, colouring-in all the unpainted space in the middle.

Halfway through our first day on the job, my little house – Wal called it 'the cabin' – was all white inside and suddenly looked more spacious than it had that morning. This happened all through the build. When the trailer arrived, it looked so small I wondered how I was going to fit my entire floor plan on it. When we put up the frame, the tiny suddenly grew into a (small) house-sized thing. When we put the bracing ply on the frame, enclosing the interior, it shrank again. Then we stuffed white insulation batts into the wall cavities and it looked bigger – and as if it'd been engulfed in a snowstorm – until we covered the insulation with plywood, and it became smaller again. I was Alice in a tiny wonderland that kept changing its dimensions all by itself.

Wal didn't talk much while he worked, except to pass on snippets of housepainter wisdom like a Zen master to a novice monk. I learned about 'fatty edges' and the 'orange peel' effect, how to tell paint was still 'green' and not ready for a second coat, how to use a hook-knife to clean the rollers. There were a couple of tense moments; a small spillage or a dropped rag could really rattle him and he'd be hard on himself on the rare occasion he made a mistake. But because I trusted him and his expertise, painting with Wal was one of the most enjoyable, and most peaceful, parts of the build.

At first, the all-white interior looked a bit clinical, without any furniture or timber features to offset its starkness. But by the last coat, the tiny was more art gallery than science lab. It was still basically a shell of a house, with nothing inside, but it looked... beautiful.

'You'll have to stop calling it "the cabin" now, Wal,' I said, as we folded his drop sheets together. 'It looks too nice to be a cabin now.'

He thought for a minute. 'I'd better call it "the penthouse" then.'

We'd created a little penthouse in the driveway.

Chapter 26

# Mind games

The irony wasn't lost on me that I was creating my new home, my penthouse-cabin, on the doorstep of a crumbling relationship. I knew it wasn't wise, but committing to the build meant, to me, committing to Max, or at least being open to learning from this whole experience. Besides, the only way out is through, as they say. Still, I sometimes found my thoughts drifting back to things Max had said to me in our early days.

If I reacted to something in a way he thought inappropriate or intense, for instance, he'd say he was 'concerned' about me. At first I teased him about how paternalistic that sounded. Then one night we were sitting on the couch after dinner at my place and he asked if I'd ever been diagnosed with a mental illness; I'd always had occasional down days and I'd seen counsellors on and off over the years, but no, I said, I'd never been told I had any kind of psychological disorder. Not long after that night, he told me about a friend of his micro-dosing with psilocybin for anxiety and suggested I look into it. Then he sent me a link to a podcast he'd listened to about borderline personality disorder.

The message was coming through: *He thinks there's something wrong with me.*

I tried to reassure myself. *This is how relationships smooth our rough edges. The person we love most in the world unearths our deepest fears, picks at the scabs of our unhealed wounds, loves us anyway and helps us outgrow them.* I wanted to believe this was happening with us.

And we did meet when I was two years into menopause and not feeling quite, or at all, myself. Like a lot of women, I was totally unprepared for this phase of my life. Even when it was happening, I didn't know what was happening. It was like flying through a cloud, understanding the physical reality while feeling completely disoriented by the experience of it.

The hot flushes came and went all day, every day. When we started sleeping together, Max would gently blow on my hot, flushing face, which didn't cool me down, but made me feel as if we were in this together. More distressing was the mental fog; I couldn't concentrate, couldn't write, would forget what I was saying mid-sentence and *why was I crying again?* I felt more anxious and insecure than at any other time in my life. And I was always saying sorry – for being more sensitive than usual, for my ups and downs, for misunderstandings with Max. It felt like a bout of PMS that had broken free of its monthly moorings and was threatening to take over my life.

I tried to learn as much as I could about menopause, to find a way through it. I quit sugar and stopped drinking coffee and alcohol, started meditating again, swam and did yoga every day, took naps when I needed to, read books and listened to podcasts about menopause, went to see a herbalist, talked to women I knew who had gone through it.

If I could just get myself together, I thought, feel steady and happy in my own skin, Max and I would be happy too. *If I was OK, we would be OK.*

It gave me hope that we could talk to each other, in the beginning. If we could talk, we could understand, I thought, and if we could understand, we could get through anything.

After a while, though, I started to notice something. Max would ask me about my issues with my dad, my family, past relationships, and I was more open and vulnerable with him than I'd been with anyone, but when I asked him personal questions he'd say he'd long ago sorted out his issues. He was 'fine'. I was always the one sharing my fears and uncertainties, while he stayed on dry land. And in the tangled ecosystem of our love, I started to believe what he seemed to: that *my* problems were the cause of *our* problems.

I wanted to trust him. But trusting him made me stop trusting myself, made me sail past red flags that had popped up in the first years of our relationship. All those times I'd felt insecure or anxious around him and dismissed my feelings as part of 'my stuff' because feeling off-balance in relationships was my normal and he kept insisting he was fine, so *what was my problem?* It didn't occur to me that our relationship could only be happy if both of us felt good inside it. Or that you don't need to have all your issues sorted out to feel loved and valued and safe. You just have to be willing to be human, together.

A few months after our ill-fated road trip and about a year before we started the build, I travelled to Turkey for a work assignment. I was there to write about a new women's trip; our all-woman group was led by a female guide, a chain-smoking academic who wore short skirts and no headscarf and loved to laugh. We drove all over Turkey meeting female winemakers and historians, chefs and boat-drivers, learning about their lives. My companions and I bonded while making Turkish coffee and being scrubbed, naked, in hammams. Feeling part of the global sisterhood soothed my aching heart, and it felt good to return to a way of being I knew so well.

But things with Max hadn't been great before I'd left and my unhappiness about us followed me there, slipped under the doors of successive hotel rooms and sneaked into bed with me. After dinner one night, I called him from my room.

We were worlds apart, not just geographically. The way he spoke to me made me feel desperately sad.

'You need help,' he said, finally, and hung up. I collapsed on the bed, feeling completely adrift. How had it come to this? How could he not know that saying 'you need help' to someone in distress, someone you love, is the opposite of helpful? In any case, where could I have sought help in the middle of the night, *in Istanbul*?

Early the next morning, exhausted from crying and lying awake all night, I saw an email from him on my phone: he'd sent me a book-length story written by one of his friends, about her nervous breakdown and subsequent stint in a psychiatric institution. He wanted me to read it. I didn't reply. But I read the book, out of curiosity, and although I felt for his friend, her experience wasn't like mine.

It was just more finger-pointing from Max, more ignoring what was going on with *us* to focus on what he saw was wrong with *me*.

When I returned from Turkey, we didn't talk about Istanbul. Or the email he'd sent. This was how it was. We couldn't talk about everything anymore. And when we did try to discuss something important, something else was always going on underneath, a mind game I could never win, even if I had known the rules.

Two months before the build, I finally asked my doctor about hormone therapy and began sticking little oestrogen patches onto my hip. The hot flushes stopped instantly, the mental clouds cleared. I could think and plan and sleep and remember things again and my moods started to stabilise.

But things still weren't right between Max and me.

When the build began and I started to back myself more, our clashes became more frequent. Max would say things that made me question myself, my memory, even my sense of reality, like:

'You're playing the victim.'

'You're in denial.'

'That's your ego talking.'

'You're not being honest with yourself.'

'You've got a chip on your shoulder.'

'You need to take responsibility for your issues.'

If I was upset, he'd blame my reaction on my 'mental health issues'. Or he'd say, after I'd started seeing Sean, '*This* is why you're seeing a therapist.'

If we disagreed, he'd accuse me of gaslighting. When I tried to tell him disagreeing wasn't gaslighting – I knew because, as Elissa Bassist says in her memoir *Hysterical*, 'a girl never forgets her first time looking up the definition of "gaslighting"', and mine had been during the build – he said *that* was gaslighting. Meanwhile he'd accuse me of not seeing things clearly or forgetting conversations we'd had. 'We decided this yesterday,' he'd say, rolling his eyes, or 'What did I tell you last week?' as if to a child. Part of me remembered exactly what we'd talked about. Another part wondered: *Had we already talked about it? Had I just forgotten?* (It was so crazy-making, I didn't stop to think: *What did it matter if I had?*

Or: *Everyone forgets things sometimes.*)

*Was this what it was like to lose your mind?*

The more he treated me as if there was something wrong with me, the more confused I felt, the more nervous I became around him, the more I forgot things, which probably only confirmed his view of me.

I tried to make sense of it all. That's what you do when someone you love behaves like this; you do mental somersaults to understand it, and what they must be feeling, to make it OK in some way, even if that means abandoning yourself and your own quite reasonable expectations for how you should be treated.

One afternoon, he was showing me how to plane a piece of wood and I started asking questions about what he was doing, to understand what I would soon be doing, which seemed to annoy him. He told me to 'show some grace'.

'OK, I'll try,' I said. 'Now let's talk about something you could do differently.' I wasn't trying to be sassy, just trying to get us back on an equal footing.

'I won't stand for this,' he said, putting down the hand-plane and walking off.

'Come on... Let's just talk, the way we used to.' It didn't have to be this hard. I knew it could be different; it *was* different sometimes.

He kept walking, back to his house. I didn't see him for the rest of the day.

There was nothing I could do to reach him when a heated moment became an hour, a whole afternoon. Sometimes he wouldn't speak to me for days. All I could do was let him be, and wait. It was like waiting for a wild animal to emerge from its den. No sudden movements, no eye contact, be patient. He would come back to me when he was ready.

Chapter 27

# A woman's place

In early January, there was a change in the psychological weather; my artist friend Jodi came to help me assemble the kitchen cabinets. As we were setting up on the first day, in Max's garage, I noticed him trying to take charge, telling me how to use the impact driver (which I'd been using for four months) and that I should finish putting in each screw using a manual screwdriver to avoid damaging the cabinetry, that it would be a 'mistake' not to glue the panels before screwing them together. I started feeling nervous and insecure.

I could see that he was trying to help, but there was an assumption beneath his words, that Jodi and I didn't know what we were doing. Because we were women? Or just less experienced than he was? I'd read about benevolent sexism, when a man (it's usually a man) does something to help someone (often a woman) because of an assumption that she's not capable of doing it herself which can, in turn, make the woman start believing she's *not* capable of doing that thing. I'd seen it in myself, too often; I'd become clumsy and forget how to do basic things when Max started to help me. I became passive. But as soon as I was alone again, my confidence would spontaneously return and I'd be able to think again.

## Building

Jodi knew her way around all types of power tools and was having none of it.

'We're fine,' she said cheerfully. 'But thanks for the advice!'

I saw something change in Max. He left us to continue our work.

'The secret,' she said, when he was gone, 'is to nod and smile, then just do it your way.'

I felt empowered watching Jodi stand up to Max that morning – without causing an argument. Of course she wasn't in an intimate relationship with him and he wasn't helping to build her home, but I knew I could learn something from it.

We talked about it over lunch that day. We bought a couple of pies and drove to the beach where we sat under a Norfolk pine tree, boots off, looking at the waves. Jodi had seen the dynamic between Max and me before, had seen how I habitually submitted to him, to keep the peace. And she'd noticed that when I *did* speak up, or suggest a different way of doing something, I did it from a position of perceived inferiority, not grounded in my own power.

I knew why: I was afraid that challenging Max would lead to an argument, because it so often did; and that was risky while I was still dependent on him for a place to finish building my home. I was also living old lessons, ones I'd learned from Mum and so many other women in my early life, lessons that had been reinforced on this build. *Keep quiet, don't ask questions, don't get in the way.*

But things were changing.

I was starting to realise I had power, too, and I was doing other things to help rebalance the situation. I was working with Sean on ways to stand my ground, in peace. I was looking after my own emotional needs – by self-soothing, pausing, listening to my body when things got tense. And

I was trying to change the way I interacted with the person I loved, by taking care of my side of the street and 'tending to the causes'; a practice I'd learned about in a Buddhist meditation group once, it involves doing what you can to move towards a goal or something you hope for, without getting attached to the outcome. *One little thing at a time.*

A few days earlier, Max and George were about to drive to Bunnings to pick up something for the build when Max came over to where I was removing nails from some old decking timber I planned to use for the deck of the tiny. I stood up from where I'd been crouching, to stretch my back and take a break.

'Sometimes you've got to just let me and Georgie do things,' he said, without preamble or explanation. I stood looking at him, letting him speak. *Tending to the causes.* But when he and George drove off, I put down my hammer and said out loud what I'd been afraid to say to Max, to hear how it would sound, like a dress rehearsal.

'Sometimes I'm going to ask questions,' I said, imagining him standing in front of me. 'Because this is my project, and it's going to be my home. And if that's irritating for you or makes you feel impatient, well, that's something for you to look at. I want us to work together peacefully, and efficiently, but that means working in a way that suits all three of us – not just you and George.'

I stood there, listening to the wind in the trees. The hurt and the anger had gone. Even if it hadn't changed the way Max spoke to me, it had felt good to get my feelings out of my head and my body, and into the air.

For three days, Jodi and I worked happily on the kitchen cabinets. After months of hearing Max tell me I was a 'pain in the arse' to work with, it felt great to work with someone else so easily. And although other female friends had helped me at various stages of the build, this felt different because Jodi was one of my closest friends. I was finally having the building-with-a-buddy experience Max and George had been having, the kind I'd wanted to have with Max.

With every cabinet we made – Jodi would line everything up and hold the pieces in place while I screwed them together using the impact driver – my confidence grew. The first cabinet took us an hour as we kept referring to the diagrams on the printed instruction sheet that came in the flat-pack, and watching how-to video clips on my phone. The second one took twenty minutes. Then we made the drawers and attached runners inside the cabinets for them to slide on.

We were 'getting things done' but within a framework of understanding, support and trust. The trust was what I appreciated most. When Jodi and I talked about how we were going to do things, she almost always understood what I said. And when we didn't understand each other, it wasn't a crisis; we'd just try again and find a way. It was such a relief, like coming home after spending too long in a country where you don't speak the language and no one speaks yours.

It was fun, too. One blazing heatwave of a day, Jodi and I worked for seven hours, attaching all the drawer fronts (ten in all) and three cabinet doors, in just our sports bras and shorts. I had to keep stopping to wipe the sweat from my eyes so I could see what I was doing. When we finished, we drove to the lake together, ran into the water fully clothed and lay on the grass afterwards, drip-drying and laughing from the sheer joy of feeling cool again.

Just as I was beginning to feel like a real tradie, I discovered something that reminded me what a newbie I still was: screws (and screwdrivers and driver heads) are *magnetised*. I could pick up a screw just by touching it with the end of my screwdriver, and it would hang there until I screwed it into a pre-drilled hole. How was I only finding out about this now, after four months on a building site? It was a tiny modern miracle.

On our last day of working together, the tiny became an all-woman zone for a change. Two of Jodi's friends called in to have a look at the tiny – Jayne, a professional housepainter, and her beekeeper partner, Sharon. While they were there, Susan, who'd helped me with the ceiling, came by to say hello. Then my friend Jacqui and her two kids arrived with a home-baked cake and some slices of fresh pineapple from their garden. Max had been shaping a surfboard in the garage all day, so I invited him to join our impromptu tea party and all was even-keeled between us. *This is how it should be*, I thought. Easy, friendly, communal. There was still plenty of build left. Maybe it could be like this in the months ahead.

But for now, this was good. This was progress.

Chapter 28

# The 'welcome home' rock

There were no date nights now or morning hugs hello. Max and I didn't speak to each other much; we didn't surf or eat or sleep together. There was no playfulness, no trust.

But the love was still there, a simmering coal we'd take turns silently coaxing back to life. I'd draw a heart on a scrap piece of wood with a builder's pencil and put it on a shelf in the garage for him to find; he'd leave a spiky spinifex seed or a sprig of wildflowers pinned to the windscreen of my car by the wiper blades. Although we both loved words, our best moments were mute; when we didn't talk, we couldn't argue.

'I know it's not easy for you, Loui,' he said one afternoon after a busy day. 'The stress of the build, menopause, not travelling, not travel writing...'

I knew he meant it kindly, but he was missing something important: I was doing OK. Some days, I did struggle and feel anxious and overwhelmed by the never-ending list of things to do. But I was getting better at managing those feelings. And mostly I was enjoying the build and coping with the daily challenges. It was as if he was reading from an old script, could only see the person I had been, not the one I was becoming.

He was also leaving himself out of the picture. The most stressful part of the build, for me, had nothing to do with the build. Just being around Max every day was the hard thing, never knowing what was going to happen next, trying to understand what was going on, trying to pretend – because who the hell had the headspace to deal with this, too? – that our relationship wasn't falling apart.

He didn't seem to realise that it was perfectly natural to feel upset when a central relationship in your life was in trouble, when someone you loved kept withdrawing all warmth and affection and interest in you and, worse, treated you as if you were mentally unwell. It was maddening sometimes, but this wasn't evidence of a mental illness; this was ordinary, everyday heartbreak.

A few days later, I woke up late after a rotten night full of wide-awake potholes, pre-dawn reading and counting backwards from a thousand in the dark. I felt almost jet-lagged, but I managed to get myself out of the house. At the beach, I had a swim, let myself cry. I didn't feel much like working, but I'd promised to meet Wal at the tiny, to pay him for the painting he'd done.

When I got there, Wal hadn't arrived yet, but I found Max working on something inside the tiny.

'Ta da,' he said, stepping back to show me that he'd finished the alcove above where my kitchen bench was going to be. Built into a niche in the wall frame and edged in scrap bits of merbau, this was where I'd planned to put fresh flowers, seed pods and autumn leaves, and small treasures I'd collected on my travels – a balsa wood jaguar from the Amazon, a family of nesting matryoshka dolls from Russia, a handmade wooden box I'd bought in Greenland with a lone kayaker on its lid.

But there was already something precious on the alcove's single shelf: a smooth grey stone, borrowed from the beach, on which Max had painted a couple of red and white flowers and the words, 'Welcome Home Loui'. The hardness between us softened, the dam of sadness burst and I hugged him, holding on for the longest time, my tears wetting his grubby workshirt. It felt good to be held. Neither of us spoke.

The rest of the day, we built on the sweetness in his gift. I was too tired to do much, so we tackled a few small jobs. Together, for a change, without arguing. At the end of the day, he offered to help me decide whether to paint the walls of my bed loft blue. I lined up some of my favourite colour cards on the window sill of the loft.

'Ready,' I said, and he climbed up the ladder to look at them with me.

But neither of us was in the mood for decisions. Instead we lay down on the bare plywood floor, our bodies close, and held hands.

'I miss this,' he said.

'Me too,' I said.

At home later that afternoon, I took a nap on the couch. When I woke up, I thought it was morning. It was 8pm. I'd slept for *four hours*. I wondered if I'd dreamed the 'welcome home' rock. But the next day, after a better sleep, I arrived at the tiny and saw it in the alcove. 'Welcome Home Loui,' it said again. I left it there for the rest of the build, to remind me of how things could be.

Chapter 29

# The notebook

It was late afternoon, in late January, and too hot to keep working. Max and I called it a day and drove to Ballina to do some errands. We'd already picked up my new fridge and were browsing the aisles of Bunnings, looking at timber panelling to make some shelves, when things started to go awry.

We'd had a minor clash earlier that day when I showed Max my latest drawings for my stairs, and the more we talked about the timber panels the smaller I felt.

'I'm finding this really difficult,' I said, eventually. 'I don't like the way you're speaking to me.' I was too tired to tease out what he meant to say and instead reacted to the way he was saying it.

'Of course you don't,' he replied, walking to the checkout without me.

In his van on the way home, I tried to take responsibility for reacting to him, told him I should have realised I wasn't in the right frame of mind to discuss or decide on shelving that day, in public. He said thanks, and nothing else.

As we pulled into his driveway, the silence broke.

We sat in the van and talked. About what had just happened, what kept happening. It felt like the last chance to say all that needed to be said, nothing off-limits, and I let everything in me pour out, all of it, too much, whatever I could think of, hoping to finally end this impasse, find a way back to us. When he went quiet, I asked him what he wanted to say, how he felt. 'I feel fine in myself,' was all he said. He reached into the glovebox, pulled out a small notebook and a pen, and started writing. As words left my lips, I saw them appear, abbreviated but unmistakeable, on the page on his lap. *He's just making notes to remember what we talked about*, I thought. But it made me feel studied. Then the talking started up again and rose and fell and rose again like a great wave and we held on and rode it to the end, which came after a long time, and sooner than I expected.

Without saying anything he got out of the van, opened the tailgate, started to unload the fridge. I got out too, tried to help. He didn't want my help, he said, before giving up, leaving the fridge half out of the van, and marching to his house. I finished what he'd started, awkwardly walking the fridge into the garage on its back corners, letting it lean on me, feeling its weight, the weight of everything.

When I went to retrieve my bag from the front of the van, I saw his notebook still sitting on the driver's seat. Without thinking, I reached over, tore out the pages he'd written while we'd been talking and put them in my bag. I knew what I did was wrong. It might have been a record of things I'd said, but these were his notes.

It's hard to remain spotless in situations like this. You endure and adapt and turn the other cheek and try to understand and be strong, but the minute you crack, and react, whatever you do or say becomes justification for the way they've acted, the things they've said. They had no choice, see what you're like, what they have to put up with? And you believe them and feel too ashamed to tell anyone, because from the outside you're the troublesome, too-emotional one and he's the good guy standing by you.

I put the notebook back where it had been. A moment later, Max was standing on the opposite side of the car, opening the driver's door, opening his notebook.

His voice was ready for war. 'Where are the notes I wrote?'

'I just want to read them.'

'If you don't give me those pages, we're through.'

I handed them over. 'Sorry,' I said.

'Now get off my land,' he said, striding back to his house again.

Driving home, feeling wrecked and numb, I realised I'd left my laptop in Max's house. Damn. I'd have to go back.

I tapped on his sliding glass door, didn't try to open it. I could see him in the kitchen. He didn't come to the door.

'I left my laptop here,' I said, through the glass, pointing to where it lay on the couch.

He walked to the couch, unlocked the door, gave me the laptop.

'We're done. I'm sorry.' Closed and locked the door again. Walked back to the kitchen.

My steadiness deserted me. 'But I gave you the pages!' I had done what he'd asked, had been doing everything I could, for so long, in so many ways, to repair what was broken between us.

I drove home in tears, peeled off my clothes, stepped into the shower, stood under the hot water, let it wash everything away until all that remained was: I was losing my home base again. But losing Mum hadn't felt like this. This had turned my world upside down and inside out, again and again, until I didn't know what was real. I'd tried to hold onto myself, hold my nerve, let things go. I'd watched my words, so clear when they left my mouth, shed their meaning before they reached him, watched everything I did become wrong in some unfathomable, unforgiveable way. I'd kept picking myself up, reassuring myself, putting my worldview right-side up again, reminding myself it was OK to *not* feel OK, and there were two of us in this. Now I was alone and feeling too much and wanting to feel nothing at all.

And I still had to finish building my little house on his land.

I felt sick.

I couldn't wash everything away. The sadness stayed. So I lit a candle, made some dinner; I needed to do ordinary, simple things. The sadness watched me, clung to me, so I let it stay, told it everything would be all right. Max and I were done, but everything would be all right.

Before I left my place the next morning, I scribbled a note to Max on a scrap of paper: *I'm sorry for my part in yesterday afternoon, for losing myself and for the hurt I caused you. Thank you for listening and trying to understand. I hope we can work together in peace. I love you.*

I'd planned to leave it on his doormat, under a stone I'd picked up on the beach, but when I reached his sliding door he was there. He opened the door. I handed him the note, and the stone, and started to walk away.

He stepped outside, read the note and looked up. 'Working together isn't the problem,' he said gruffly. 'It's *being* together.'

I turned back to him. I had nothing left. 'Can I see those notes you made yesterday?'

'I've typed them up. I'll email them to you,' he said, going inside again.

'Thanks.'

Sitting on a milk crate in the tiny half an hour later, I read his email on my phone.

There was a brief introduction that read like a clinical assessment, saying that what followed was an example of what happens when I have 'heightened anxiety attacks' and that he'd been 'conciliatory and supportive' during our talk. Below that was a list of about twenty statements he said were my 'exact words'. I recognised three of them. The rest he'd disfigured completely, turning a desperate and sincere sharing into bitterness and blame.

This is something therapists and relationship experts don't always tell you: communication isn't just about what you say, it's about what the other person hears. You can use all the 'I' statements you like, speak about your own experience, keep your voice low and quiet, refrain from blaming – and the other person might still hear accusations or blame, to make your words match how *they* feel and their own perception of the situation.

As Max stepped into the tiny, I held up my phone, his email still open on its screen. 'This isn't what I said.'

'Well, I wrote down your words exactly as you said them,' he replied. 'You probably can't remember what you said because you were hysterical.'

There it was. The word that says more about the person speaking, and the world we live in, than the person being spoken about. A word that dismisses and minimises. A gendered word. *Men get angry, women get hysterical.*

Nothing I'd said the day before had reached him. In that moment, the anger I'd felt evaporated, leaving behind a cold clarity that the person I had loved for almost four years was unwilling or just unable to find a way through this impasse. His need to be right, by making me wrong, was stronger than any desire he might have had to reconnect.

All I could do was keep working.

I'd planned to finish making a feature wall in my day loft that morning, from the smooth shiplap cedar left over from cladding the front of the tiny. A few days earlier I'd measured and cut the nine and a half planks I needed and decided what order I'd put them up on the wall – but faced with the task now, after the emotional tornado of the day before, I suddenly felt incapable of doing it.

I wasn't up to precision work. Or another 'fucking first time' (as vulnerability guru Brené Brown calls them). I could have postponed this job. Maybe I should have. But I wanted something to do. I wanted, just for a day, not to feel.

So I swallowed my pride and asked Max to help me. I'd still have the satisfaction of finishing the task I'd started. And maybe this little project would be a balm for our sore hearts. I was surprised when he agreed.

All that morning we kneeled on the floor of the day loft, surrounded by cedar planks, boxes of nails and our two hammers, close enough to touch, without touching. Starting at the top – for a neat finish on the most visible part of the wall – we took turns holding each cedar plank snug against the one above it and nailing it in place, making the nails flush by tapping them with a hammer and the nail-punch.

It took all my concentration just to hammer the nails in straight. My confidence was at an all-time low. I found myself letting Max do things I knew I could do. One of my heroes, solo sailor Liz Clark, who spent ten years sailing alone across the Pacific, would have found a way to do what needed doing herself, I thought. And maybe I could have summoned the energy to do that too, if I'd been alone in the middle of an ocean, instead of in the middle of a breakup sitting right next to the person I'd just broken up with.

But we did it. Plank by plank, the cedar crept down the little wall, transforming it into something beautiful. The final touch was edging the wall on each side with two vertical strips of reclaimed merbau. It had only taken a morning, and forever.

At lunchtime that day, we sat on stools at a bench on his verandah and ate our sandwiches in silence until he said, 'I'm all ears if you want to talk.'

I didn't feel like talking. But I did have something to say.

'I think I understand now why you're always saying I don't take responsibility for my issues. It's because when I say how I feel, you hear me blaming you. Those notes you took say more about you than about me. Most of the things on that list I didn't say.'

He insisted, again, that I'd said everything he'd written down, believed he was right, started getting stirred up again. 'I'm done,' he said, standing up and turning to walk back into the house. I knew he wasn't talking about finishing his lunch.

'OK. But this is no way to end it,' I said. Calm, steady. *Let's remember the love between us, respect each other, do this properly.*

He put down his plate and flopped into the black armchair beside me. He looked as depleted as I was.

'Can I sit with you?' I said. More formal than usual, careful.

'Sure,' he said. Non-committal, cool.

I squeezed in next to him and he put his arms around me. I rested my head against his chest. So this was it. The end of us.

'I feel relieved,' he said.

'Me too,' I said.

We sat like that for a long time, in this new place we'd arrived at, saying nothing, all our words having been discarded on the way there.

'Want to shake this off?' I said. We did this sometimes, mid-argument, to bring us back to our physical reality and release tension, as prey animals do after a close call with a predator.

'You can,' he said quietly.

I got up out of the chair and shook my hair out of its ponytail and flapped my arms, jiggled my legs, swirled my hips and started to feel the sadness lift, started to feel lighter, surprised myself by smiling.

He looked up at me, the love in his eyes again. 'I still want us to hang out, go back to being friends.' There he was, the one I'd missed and still loved.

I climbed back onto the armchair and nestled close to him.

'Everything will be OK,' I whispered into his neck, not really knowing what 'OK' looked like anymore.

Chapter 30

# Love and architraves

When I arrived at the tiny early the next day, Max greeted me with a smile, a hug and a kiss. He asked how I was feeling after yesterday.

'I feel... good,' I said. 'You?'

'Good. Kinda feels like the pressure's off, doesn't it?'

'Yeah.' I smiled. 'Careful, I might cry again.'

'That's OK, bub,' he said.

Warmth, kindness, understanding. The love tap was 'on' again and while that might have been confusing after all that had happened over the past few days, it felt too good to question.

All day he was more affectionate, more present than he'd been in ages. And I felt more self-assured and more solid in myself. Days like this I didn't lose myself in him; I could hold onto my way of seeing things, even when it was different from his. I was free again – and still loved. *Was this what I'd had to learn? Was our relationship finally becoming what we'd both wanted it to be? Did we have to break up to find it? Could we sustain this?*

It turned out to be one of the best days of the entire build.

It probably helped that Wal was on-site. And that we were finishing a major job – making the architraves – which always felt good.

First, I sanded all the architraves. It was Wal's job to paint them so he followed me around the tiny, a paintbrush in one hand and a small pot of Lexicon Quarter semi-gloss in the other, until we ran out of architraves to sand and paint. Max and I decided to make the last two together – the architraves framing the two big kitchen windows above my kitchen bench – and we agreed he'd wear the boss's cap. That felt more democratic than him just taking charge. Besides, he knew what to do, I wanted to learn and when our roles were clear, there was no power struggle.

I measured the windows and cut the correct lengths we needed, angling the dropsaw to 45 degrees so we could make 'mitre-cut' corners. Then we started nailing these strips to the walls, 'framing' each window.

After deferring to Max too much on the cedar wall the day before, I'd got my mojo back. I felt confident again, and creative. One of the first things that surprised me about building was how creative it is; a build is basically a never-ending sequence of problems, coming at you all day every day, in search of clever solutions. Putting up the architraves, I had to find a way to avoid denting them while hammering them to the walls, because I wasn't as steady-handed with a hammer as Max was. (One dent wasn't a problem, but an architrave pock-marked with them would have required filling and sanding, slowing down the whole 'finishing the tiny' process.)

So I made a cardboard collar – a piece of cardboard with a hole in the middle – which I slipped over the head of each nail before I hammered it into place. It was a drop in the ocean of problems we had to solve during the build, but figuring it out felt good. And it was another lesson in finding a way to do something that suited me, my body and my level of experience – just as Sophie had taught me – instead of trying to do it the way Max might have and giving up or getting frustrated because I couldn't.

After we finished the architraves, it was time to install the kitchen cabinets in the tiny. There were eight of them, all heavy even without their drawers and doors, and it was awkward carrying them from the garage, up the tiny's makeshift 'steps' and in through the door – and still Max and I didn't argue.

We didn't even argue when we had to make sure the cabinets were all level, which involved one of us (me) lying on the floor and reaching under each cabinet to twist its four legs while the other (Max) issued instructions from above, like 'Lower at the back' and 'Higher in the front right corner'. We also had to finalise the height of the cabinets and benches – a process that saw me pretending to wash dishes and cut vegetables to check what height was right for me and running to Max's kitchen a few times to check the height of *his* benches – and, again, everything went smoothly.

We discussed things, we understood each other, we barely disagreed. It was as if a spell had been broken and now, at last, we could communicate.

Our final job for the day was to remove any debris from the long gap we'd left between the plywood floor under the cabinets on each side of the tiny and the main hardwood floor in the middle (this gap would allow the hardwood planks to expand and contract with changes in temperature and humidity) in preparation for installing the kickboards at the base of the cabinets.

Crawling on our hands and knees, we poked screwdrivers into the gap and found long lost bits of insulation that looked like miniature cotton balls. We fished out leaves and small sticks that had fallen into the tiny before we'd put the roof on. And assorted nails, staples and screws we'd used at various stages of the build. Even a long-deceased gecko, dried and skeletal.

'This is like an archaeological dig,' I said, lifting out another screw that clung to the tip of my screwdriver. 'All these relics from the past four and a half months of our build.'

Max sat up and looked at me. 'I love it when you say it's *our* build.'

That surprised me. I'd started to think he didn't care anymore, about me or the build. 'It *is* our build, babe. We've done it together every step of the way. Lots of blood, sweat and tears in this little house,' I said.

'More tears than blood maybe.' His eyes crinkled into a smile.

It was late afternoon and ridiculously humid, so we decided to end our day with a swim at the lake, together. Another thing we hadn't done in a while.

Standing at the water's edge, slightly ahead of me, Max turned around. 'Are we doing a swim or just having a dip?' In that moment, I didn't mind what we did. I just loved that he was asking. Everything I had ever wanted was in that question.

'I think, a dip,' I said. We swam out a little way, side by side, the water clean and cool, and returned to the shallows where we frolicked in the black-tea water and giggled like children. Or lovers. Without thinking, I wrapped my arms and legs around him as if he were a skinny, half-submerged tree. He put his arms around me and held me close. I tried to enjoy the moment, just as it was, without wishing for anything more, but back at his place he invited me to stay for dinner and while the rice was cooking we had a shower together and – both of us too weary to resist – ended up in his loft, still naked, making love. Passionate, loving, sexy love, after a whole day of what felt like foreplay. I let myself be carried along by it all, the longing in me satisfied and happy and not letting go, not yet.

Lovely though the architrave day had been, I wasn't under any illusions that Max and I were back together. But I was glad he still seemed as committed to the build as I was. We settled into a new routine, ticking off small jobs two by two – because we were working separately now. While I screwed the kitchen cabinets together, he made a privacy screen for my outdoor shower out of old railway sleepers. While I painted the bathroom door (blue), he started measuring up the timber slab that was to become my bench top.

Still, nothing had been resolved, so nothing had really changed between us. I still had a knot in my stomach as I drove to his place each morning, never sure what the day might bring: sunshine or thunderstorms. And every day, I would fail in some way, in my own eyes or in Max's. I could spend whole days failing, from the moment I put on my toolbelt. I failed for being too anxious, too self-critical, too serious, too sensitive to the way Max spoke to me. For caring too much, knowing too little, taking too long to make decisions, being too cocky *and* not confident enough.

I'd drive home feeling exhausted from the effort of just trying to get through the day without capsizing. Some days I did capsize. But I was learning to right myself too. When I lived in Japan, there was a proverb I'd hear all the time: 'Fall down seven times, get up eight' (*nana korobi, ya oki*). At first, I thought, *That doesn't make sense*; if you fall down seven times, you only have to get up seven times, not eight. Eventually I learned that it's like a koan, a Zen riddle that can be understood only by sitting with it, not thinking about it. Then it made perfect sense: the 'getting up' times outnumber the 'falling down' times when your resilience becomes greater than the trials you've faced. Perseverance could be its own reward.

## Building

I could keep getting up, keep doing everything I could to keep the build on track, to keep things harmonious with Max. I could love, without expecting love in return. These were things I could control. There was a simplicity in that, and a sense of trust. The rest was out of my hands.

Chapter 31

# **Butterflies**

Before we'd started the build, Max and I had visited a timber mill up the coast where I chose a great slab of white gum, almost 4 metres long and as wide as a kitchen counter, for the timber bench that would run along one side of the tiny.

I loved that the slab had come from an old tree that had been salvaged from a windbreak on a nearby dairy farm; it had been cut down and milled on the spot. But when the sawmill guy lifted the tarp under which it had been drying for a year, I had to squint to imagine it as a beautiful timber bench – it was grey and coarse with uneven, splintery edges. (Freshly cut wood needs to dry out so it's stable enough to use; otherwise whatever you make with it can warp and crack, responding like a living tree to changes in the weather.)

It looked slightly better when it was delivered a few months later, having been 'dressed' and 'thicknessed' (more new building terms), but it was going to take a bit of work for it to even resemble a bench. I told Max I wanted to do it. Being a single piece of wood – no corners, no joins – I thought it'd be a relatively straightforward, if time-consuming, project, and I wanted to put some of my woodworking skills to use again and make my own 'kitchen table'.

Soon after that, one afternoon in February, I returned from visiting Dad again to find Max in the garage, dust mask and earmuffs on, electric planer in hand, working on the slab. I felt a prickle of annoyance; I was glad he'd started on the bench, but it bothered me that he'd started without me, and without letting me know. He stopped the noisy planer and removed his earmuffs to say hello, but when I reminded him I wanted to work on the slab, he put his earmuffs on again and got back to work.

I figured I'd get my chance.

But I didn't. He worked on the slab every day for two weeks and the more I saw him enjoying the work, the less I wanted to step in. Maybe I was still thinking like one half of a couple, suppressing my own desires to keep him happy. Maybe it was simpler than that. He was making a bench for me, and I was letting him do something I'd wanted to do; two silent acts of love running side by side towards the same finish line.

Making a bench out of a piece of wood turned out to be a major undertaking. I'd had no idea. There were so many phases to it: planing out the chainsaw grooves, sanding the top and bottom with increasingly fine grades of sandpaper, removing bark from the slab's 'live edge' before sanding smooth its curves, filling cracks in the timber with epoxy resin (which made Max's garage smell like a surfboard factory or a boatyard), waiting for the resin to set then sanding those bits too... It was endless.

Max also made about twenty wooden 'butterfly joints'. Each one was about an inch long and looked like a little bow tie. The plan was for him to make little bow-tie-shaped grooves at both ends of all the cracks in the slab and glue these 'butterflies' into them, like wooden mosaic tiles – to stop the slab splitting further along its natural fault lines. I loved the butterfly idea. But while they stabilised the slab, they caused another rift between us.

When we'd first talked about it, I thought Max planned to make the butterflies from bits of white gum, so they'd be the same colour as the bench and blend in. But the next day he called me into the garage to show me the butterflies he'd started making – out of leftover merbau, a darker, redder wood. I liked them.

A couple of days later, he had another idea. He wanted to cut timber knots out of surplus pieces of cedar and put them *on top* of the merbau butterflies for a more 'natural' look; only the woody knots would be visible, running along the spine of the slab. I wasn't sold on it, told him I preferred the simplicity of the merbau butterflies, which would look like a visible mend, like hand-sewn patches on a favourite pair of jeans. It seemed less honest, somehow, to hide the butterfly joints that were really holding the slab together.

It made me think about homes and other structures I'd seen on my travels, places that looked as if they'd grown out of their surroundings, almost of their own accord. Stone walls in Scotland and Portugal that really were made of stones, carried from the nearby fields. Mud-brick huts made of mud, water and straw, their earthen floors actual bare earth, swept clean by brooms that were just bundles of sticks. In Cambodia, I watched a father and his teenage sons re-thatch the roof of the family hut with fresh green palm fronds they'd cut from the rainforest around them. On the island of Bali, I walked barefoot through an architect-designed stilt house, one of a dozen or so made entirely of bamboo inhabiting a wooded river valley as if they'd always been there.

It was comforting, on some elemental level, for a built thing to be what it appeared to be. No trickery, no subtext. And it made me want to resist, in my own tiny house, as much as was modernly possible, clever materials masquerading as something else – vinyl flooring that looked like hardwood, timber-composite cladding made to resemble weatherboard planks, slate-like shingles made of recycled plastic.

Max knew more about woodwork than anyone I knew and I wanted to trust his judgement, but I was the one who was going to be using this bench every day. More than any other feature in the tiny, I wanted to get it right. I asked him to show me the cedar knots before we made a decision. He said he would.

Early the next day, while Max was surfing, I wandered over to where the slab was resting on two sawhorses and noticed that he'd already glued some of the merbau butterflies into place. I didn't know if that meant he'd decided to use the butterflies by themselves after all – or if he was still planning to put the cedar knots on top of them – but I liked their rustic simplicity, the fact that they were all slightly different shapes and sizes because Max had cut them out by hand.

'Hey, the merbau butterflies look great,' I said, walking over to him as soon as he returned from the beach. I was happy, the bench was looking good, it was a beautiful day. 'Let's just stick with that and *not* overlay them with the cedar knots, yeah? What do you think?'

I thought he'd be pleased. I was being positive and clear about what I liked, showing my appreciation for what he'd done *and* saving him extra work.

He was not pleased. 'So you've changed your mind.'

'No... We hadn't made a decision yet.' I hadn't forgotten our agreement.

'We agreed to use the cedar knots. You're micro-managing me.'

We walked over to the bench. He'd made the merbau butterflies rough, he explained, because he'd planned to cover them with the cedar knots. If he'd known the butterflies were going to be visible, he would have made them look neater.

So he'd decided to use the cedar knots, without showing them to me first as we'd agreed. And accused me of changing the plan.

'I really appreciate all the work you've put in on the slab, babe.' I wiggled my toes inside my workboots to keep myself grounded. 'You've done so much and I love it.' I touched one of the merbau butterflies; it was still tacky from the resin.

'I just wish you'd trust me to make it beautiful,' he said, before walking away to hang his dripping wetsuit on the clothesline. End of discussion.

We didn't talk about the merbau butterflies or the cedar knots again that day or any other day, but he left the butterflies in, as I'd asked.

Two days later, George came to help Max put the slab in place, a technical job that involved making detailed cuts in one side of it where it would slot under the two kitchen windows. I'd made a 4-metre-long cardboard template for them to use, showing where the cuts needed go, but as soon as George arrived, I was ushered out of the way and it became the Max and George Show again.

It didn't help that I didn't know how to be around Max anymore. We weren't partners. There was too much emotion swirling around for us to be friends. We were barely workmates.

What did help was that I understood better now why social exclusion can hurt so much, even when it doesn't come on top of other hurts: because we're social creatures whose very survival once depended on being part of a group. Being excluded was dangerous, so our bodies and minds, over millions of years, developed mechanisms to avoid it, and to react when it happened. It's biological, evolutionary, natural. Even just a short stint of feeling left out can apparently release stress hormones, raise our heart rates and put our brains into a hypervigilant state. I was living proof of that.

I'd also started writing myself 'no bloody wonder' letters. This is one of the exercises Sarah Wilson recommends in *First we make the beast beautiful*, her book about anxiety, and it became one of my go-to ways to steady myself. It involves writing down challenging aspects of the situation you're in – working with your ex every day, say, while building your first home, something you've never done before, on his land, in the middle of a global pandemic – and acknowledging that it was perfectly understandable to find that situation challenging. In other words, *no bloody wonder* you feel stressed.

I knew how to take care of myself now, too. So I spent the day George joined us on a side project of my own: sanding a piece of cypress pine I'd rescued from a building site (I was planning to turn it into an outdoor seat), while listening to interesting podcasts. And I took myself out for lunch, to the lake. It felt indulgent to spend a whole hour, when there was still so much to do, lazing on the grass in the shade, eating a sandwich and reading a book, but I needed this. Time alone, time in nature, time away.

I arrived back at the tiny feeling more grounded and relaxed than I had in days, just in time to see Max and George slide my timber bench into position on top of the cabinets Jodi and I had made.

'It looks amazing,' I said, before thanking Max and George for doing such a great job. They seemed happy with the way it had turned out. Except for one thing: Max was still embarrassed about how rustic the butterfly joints looked. But I loved them. Because they were honest. And because they were imperfect, like us.

Soon after that, George left for the day, Max went out and I started tidying up our worksite. I carried the power tools they'd been using back to the garage and put them back in their cases, coiled up the extension leads that trailed like umbilical cords between the tiny and the garage every day now, swept up all the sawdust in the tiny.

I was just about to pull down the roller door on the garage when I noticed something on Max's workbench: a small pile of cedar knots, about twenty of them, all carefully cut from leftover pieces of cedar cladding. I hadn't known Max had actually made the cedar knots, hadn't realised how beautiful they would be. There were sepia swirls and cocoa-coloured galaxies and kohl-rimmed eyes. *When had he made these? Why hadn't he told me or shown them to me?* Now they lay on the bench, unneeded. I suddenly wanted to cry.

It all felt too hard, too sad, this whole situation, working together and not being together, everything unresolved filling the air between us. I still loved the merbau butterflies, was still happy with the end result, but I didn't love the way we'd reached it.

That night I sent Max a message, thanking him again for all his hard work that week, telling him again how much I loved the butterfly joints and apologising for my part in our misunderstanding about the cedar knots. 'I'm sorry you couldn't do them the way you'd planned to,' I said.

'Thanks Loui,' he replied.

Then I shed my dirty workclothes and stood under the shower for a long time, letting all the sadness, about everything, pour out of me.

Chapter 32

# Confused gratitude

I didn't think it would be this way, that so much of this build would be entangled in the relationship that padded along beside it on its own very different trajectory. Every structural element we worked on became infused with whatever was going on between Max and me. Every plywood wall, every architrave, every floorboard. Everything around us had its own stories and memories.

At the same time, the practical simplicity of what we were doing each day, the undeniable properties of the materials we were working with, seemed to ease the emotional ups and downs. My little house was like a ship at sea, one with multiple masts and acres of sail, holding her course, making steady progress – and keeping me steady, despite the changeable weather beyond her gunwales.

It had been a typical wet-season week – the days and nights hot, humid and still – and I was content to be inside, out of the sun, sanding and sealing the floors of the two lofts. When it was time to tackle the hardwood floor, my first job was to make up some epoxy, which involved mixing five parts resin with one part hardener in a plastic cup ('521' was helpfully written on both bottles), before dabbing and dripping the sticky mixture into the floor's cracks and knots to prevent them scratching bare feet or snagging socks when I moved into the tiny. Then I had to wait for it to harden. In this weather, that could take a couple of days. Sometimes the first batch of resin wouldn't quite fill a crack and I'd have to mix up, and dab on, some more. And wait again.

Just as wood contracts and expands and warps and twists with changes in temperature and humidity, resin sets when it sets. You couldn't argue with such a natural truth, and I found that immeasurably reassuring.

When all the resin spots finally dried, I started on the sanding. I'd bought some heavy-duty black kneepads especially for this job (it was money well spent; they don't call it *hard*wood for nothing), which went well with the rest of my ensemble: orange earmuffs, a face mask (no safety goggles as they kept fogging up), an old T-shirt and shorts, and thick socks (no boots allowed inside during Floor Week, and bare feet might have left dirty marks on the floor). With my safety gear on, I got to work.

It was such a workout just holding onto the belt sander – it has a sandpaper 'belt' like the tread on a tank, which spins really fast – I had to tie a bandanna around my head to stop sweat dripping from my brow onto the freshly sanded floor. But I loved this job, loved the muffled noise, and feeling my arms vibrating with the buzzing belt sander as I kneeled on the floor, pushing it forward and back, forward and back, parallel to the floorboards, calmly and literally 'going with the grain'.

Mostly, I loved seeing the results of my labour as I worked. For four days, the interior of the tiny was engulfed in a dust-blizzard as I sanded away years of accumulated grime. The floorboards had been in a shed beside Max's garage for almost fifteen years and when we'd first nailed them in place that first week of the build, they'd looked almost black, but the more I sanded, the more the blackbutt showed its true colours – burnt oranges and bushfire blacks, clear blondes and moody browns – and I fell in love with my hardwood floor for the second time.

Meanwhile, Max made two boat-inspired floor hatches – each one consisting of twelve hardwood planks attached to a piece of plywood – to cover the underfloor storage spaces between the axles of the trailer (we'd temporarily covered these gaping holes in the floor with plywood during the build so we could safely walk around). This was to be my she-shed, a place to store all my camping gear, my hiking boots and backpacks, my winter clothes (in summer, and my summer clothes in winter), boxes of old photos and paperwork I rarely needed to access (like my passport, a little pandemic joke).

The finishing touch was a marine-grade stainless steel ring-pull on each hatch, completing the nautical look. Max had done a beautiful job. But when he lowered them into place, he pointed out a problem: each hatch had a slight dip in it – one hatch lifted up at its edges, the other bowed in the middle – and made a loose-floorboard sound every time I stepped on it. It didn't bother me. Those wonky floor hatches were like the butterfly joints: beautiful because of, not despite, their imperfections and idiosyncrasies, like the people we love. It was another bit of the tiny that would have its own story.

The last day of Floor Week was a 10-hour epic. I finished the sanding, then cleaned and oiled the entire floor, including the two hatches, just on dark, my sense of achievement dimmed by the fact that it was my birthday the next day and Max hadn't mentioned it. He usually loved celebrating other people's birthdays.

I was cleaning my oily brushes when I saw him get into his van and start reversing out of the garage. I walked over. His driver's window was open.

'Do you want to do something with me tomorrow?' I wasn't sure what I wanted him to say, if I even wanted to spend my birthday with him.

'I don't know,' he said, before driving away.

I finished packing up. I felt numb. I knocked on Katie's door, to ask her for a plastic bag to store the oily rags I'd used on my floor, secretly hoping for some human warmth.

'Hello!' she said, opening her door. Smiling, friendly. My shoulders relaxed. She disappeared into her kitchen in search of a plastic bag – and returned holding a Tupperware container as well.

'I made you some dinner because you worked so late,' she said, handing it over.

I was so touched by her kindness, I burst into tears. She wrapped me in a hug.

'It's been a long day,' I said, wiping my face.

'I know it's hard,' she said, understanding more than I could have explained in that moment, something else I was grateful for.

My fifty-sixth birthday was my original, hoped-for, move-in date, but when it sailed by, I felt surprisingly OK about that. I was slowly realising that every build follows its own timeline. Nothing personal, just the way it is. I'd been comparing this build to a long trip without noticing that, like any trip, it would follow its own rules. As John Steinbeck wrote in *Travels with Charley*, about his 1960 road trip across America with his eponymous poodle, a journey is like a marriage: the sure way to be wrong about it is to believe you can control it.

I'd had plenty of firsthand experience of this. On one of my most memorable journeys, a three-month overland trip across Africa with twenty strangers, we ran out of food in Burkina Faso, I was almost killed by a drunk taxi driver in Cameroon, half of us (including me) got malaria in Zaire (now the Congo) – and I rolled with it all, didn't once come unstuck. Life at home always seemed the harder game, maybe because I expected it to run smoothly, because it was supposed to be the gap between difficult things, or because I was never sure where it was taking me. So I kept going away, distilling life to a sketchy itinerary and whatever I could fit into a backpack. And tried not to think about why I couldn't, or didn't want to, stay in one place.

I hadn't been missing travelling itself – the build was exciting enough – but I missed the way I often felt when I travelled: open, curious, ready for anything. Too often during the build I felt afraid of change, which was unfortunate considering that my whole world was now a vortex of major life changes.

So my birthday gift to myself was a day off, the kind of day off you have when you're travelling and you're tired of sightseeing and want to just relax and be where you are. Max sent me a message that morning to tell me there were a few 'little surprises' waiting for me at his place, but I needed a day off from him, too. I kept the day simple – a swim in the sea, a leisurely lunch with Dad, a nap, a few chats with friends I'd neglected for five months – and went to bed that night feeling peaceful, loved and accepted, just as I was.

The next morning, I arrived at Max's place just as he and his Japanese friend Mori arrived after having an early surf together. I was still feeling calm and I liked Mori, always felt at ease around him; sometimes I tried speaking Japanese with him. But as we all walked into Max's house together, Max seemed distracted and short-tempered. I noticed my birthday presents on his dining table, but decided to wait for him to give them to me.

He went straight to the kitchen and started making breakfast for Mori.

'Are you going to give me my presents?' I asked, playfully. Like a good dog, waiting for the nod before wolfing down the snack balanced on her nose.

'I'm not going to play games with you,' Max said.

So I sat down at the table and, while he and Mori chatted in the kitchen, silently unwrapped the presents: a new wetsuit top for surfing, a calendar Max had made using photos from the build, and a beautiful set of wooden spoons he'd carved from various woods we'd used in the tiny – cedar, merbau, white gum, pine. I went to the kitchen, thanked him with a hug, told him I loved the presents, the wooden spoons most of all, but he was still far away. His beautiful, thoughtful gifts, so full of love and care, didn't match the experience of receiving them.

That feeling of confused gratitude had permeated the entire build. Did the gifts, the generous acts, tell the real story, or the way they were given? Which one should I have believed?

I was caught in that bind all day.

We managed to work together, just. Installed a pine shelving unit Max had made for my kitchen. Attached the bathroom basin to the wall. Planned the boxes that would contain the downlights above the kitchen bench.

But being around him wore me down. The mixed signals and crossed wires, the body language disagreeing with the spoken words. After working alone for most of that week, I felt disoriented again. Everything I did was wrong. No matter what I did or how I did it, Max seemed irritated, and resentful.

'I can't do this anymore,' he finally said, at lunchtime, and drove off, taking all his power tools with him. I guessed he was going to work at George's house, but I needed some of those tools, so my work day ended there.

I always tried to expect the unexpected when I drove to Max's place, to prepare myself for how things might be, but the next day was unexpected in a new way: he wasn't home. He hadn't sent me a message to say he would be at George's or anywhere else that day, or when he'd be back. And he still had all the tools. I didn't try to contact him. I let him be.

It was unnerving not knowing when Max was going to show up, or how things would be when he did. But it turned into a good day. The electrician, Allan, came to install all my power points and light switches in the tiny. A couple of friends popped in and stayed for a chat. A package arrived from my travel writer mentor and friend, John, from Sydney: a small bottle of sparkling wine with a note that said, 'For the upcoming launch of the good ship *Tiny*'. And after Allan finished up and left, I rode my bike to the lake to swim and sit in the shade of the paperbarks.

That night, I sent Max a message. 'Hi babe, are you OK?'

He replied straight away, said he was OK, asked if the electrical work was all done. We sent a few careful messages back and forth. There was no warmth, no explanation, but he said he'd see me at the tiny the next day.

Chapter 33

# An end in sight

I gave my landlady a month's notice at my rented studio and set a move-in date, for late March. The tiny wouldn't be finished by then, but it would be habitable, I hoped. Just having a deadline felt good, after months of inching towards an end point without knowing when we might reach it.

That's when I noticed an unexpected feeling swimming against the tide of everything we'd been doing. Shopping for taps and kitchen handles at Bunnings one afternoon, wearing my filthy work clothes and dirty boots, knowing my way around the aisles now, feeling at ease around the hardware, it hit me: *I don't want this to be over.*

I mean, I wanted everything to be done. I wanted to move into my beautiful little house and move on with my life. And I was feeling the fatigue of almost six months of decision-making and on-the-job training. But a big part of me loved that the build had taken over my life. I loved the way it simplified things, gave me direction, made everything unrelated to it fade into the background. And as long as I was absorbed in the daily ritual of getting through my to-do list, I could avoid making any big decisions about My Life and what came next. That was a big unknown. Beyond the outer limits of our small town, borders were still closed, lockdowns were in place, restrictions on social activities came and went, and I had no job or assignments waiting for me.

So I tried to make the most of the last few weeks, not realising that the build wasn't done with me – and wouldn't be for a while yet.

Two weeks before move-in day, meaning we had just two weeks to finish a few features I'd really need to live in the tiny, Max went camping for a week with some mates. At first I was annoyed. We still had *so* much to do.

It was only when he left that I realised: I needed a break too.

I'd been working on the tiny six days a week, sometimes seven, for six months, all through summer, with the heat and the humidity and the rain and the emotional tension. So for the first few days, I had my own mini-break, in situ. There were leisurely lake swims and surf sessions, impromptu chats at the beach. There might have been a massage; there were definitely afternoon naps.

When I got back into work mode, the relaxed feeling lingered; I got things done, without feeling stressed about them. I oiled the merbau frame around the little alcove above the timber bench, and the merbau planks edging the two lofts. Screwed the laminated bench onto the cabinets on the sink side of the kitchen, which involved folding myself into the doorless cabinets like a magician's assistant to reach the tight corners at the back. Attached a little strip of flashing above where my front door would soon be, to shield it from the rain. Used a tiny watchmaker's screwdriver to install 'finger pulls' on the (still to be installed) bathroom door. And reversed the hinges on my new fridge (and learned that most single-door fridges have their hinges on the right; who knew?).

The week ended with Allan, the electrician, returning for another full day's work. While I pottered around, he put in the last of the power points and all my wall-mounted lights – eleven in all, which seemed excessive for a house only 7 metres long until I learned that lights can create different 'zones' in a tiny, so you don't feel like you're living in a single room – and the cutest little 'switchboard' I'd ever seen, neatly inset into the wall under one end of my timber bench.

It had been a gloomy day and the tiny was still very basic inside – a timber bench running down one side, a dark grey bench on the other side of the galley kitchen, no built-in furniture yet – but late that afternoon we passed another small milestone. Allan stepped outside and trailed an extension cord from my tiny's caravan-like power outlet across the driveway to the garage.

'Ready?' he called out, standing at the switch.

'Ready!' I replied from inside.

My little house suddenly came alive. I'd probably never again have all the lights on at once, but it was a beautiful sight. I ran outside and gave a little yelp of joy. If I squinted, my tiny looked just like a cabin, one that was taller and had more windows than the one in Norway but looked just as inviting, as if beckoning me inside after a day's wanderings in the forest.

The day after Max returned from his camping trip, I needed his help cutting some screws with the pliers; the ones that came with the kitchen cabinets were too long. I'd tried to cut them myself, but I didn't have the strength to grip the pliers hard enough. As I walked to his house I remembered something Liz Clark, the solo sailor, had said in her memoir, *Swell*: sometimes a girl just needs some man-muscle to help her do something. Besides, it was a small job; it would only take Max a few minutes.

I found him reading on his verandah. He lowered his book while I explained what I needed. Without having seen the screws, he said they didn't need cutting; I must be doing something wrong. We got into a verbal tussle.

'What's up?' I said.

'Well, you seem anxious all the time,' he said.

'Right now, I'm just frustrated.' I tried to stay focused on why I was there. 'I want to finish this job and I need your help to do that.'

'George and I would have finished the build *two months ago* if it wasn't for you,' he said, raising his book again to hide his face. Over and out.

On the outside, same old argument. But inside, something was different. Arguing with Max still stirred me up physically – my body couldn't help reacting to the escalating tension, what it perceived as a threat – but I could sense something unshakeable in me, too. No matter how much work he'd done on this build, how much he'd done to help me, his attitude towards me didn't have to determine how I saw myself. I don't know whether it was the therapy, the yoga, the meditation or any of the other things I'd been doing that helped in that moment. Or the fact that the build was nearing its end. Maybe I was just more comfortable with being uncomfortable now, able to feel nervous *and* back myself at the same time. Whatever the reason, I was making headway in choppy waters that previously might have sunk me.

I resisted the urge to ask Max how to do things after that, and my solo work days just before I moved in taught me more about the way I liked to work, the way I worked best, than all those months of working alongside him and George.

One job that took me a full day was screwing the handles on the kitchen cabinet doors and drawers. (Max finally looked at the screws, agreed they *did* need to be shortened and kindly cut them for me.) There were fourteen handles in all, little black Ds that would be horizontal on the drawers and vertical on the cabinets. The preparation was tedious: walking back and forth between the tiny and the garage, gathering all the tools I'd need, setting up a laser level on a tripod I'd borrowed from Jodi to line up the handles. I felt nervous. Although it was a small job, mistakes at this stage of the build would have been an expensive, time-wasting hassle.

But I knew what to do. I measured where the handles had to go and made sure they all lined up with those on neighbouring cabinets, like balconies on an apartment block. I drilled holes and manually, carefully, screwed the handles in place from inside each drawer or door. And I breathed, took breaks and watched YouTube videos whenever I felt stuck.

By mid-afternoon it was done. The handles looked as if they belonged where they were – as if the result hadn't come after a dozen decisions and revisions and a day's worth of pernickety tinkering. Considering the scale of the task, my sense of achievement was wildly oversized, but it was just right for the rookie I still was, after all.

⌂

With my move-in date mere days away and George on holiday, Max and I enlisted another builder friend to help with a few last technical jobs we couldn't do on our own. Kramer was a gentle giant, always up for a chat and caring to a fault. On the rare occasion he wore a shirt, usually in winter, it was a joyous Hawaiian print that matched his affable personality; he liked to say he was 'seventy-five per cent female'. Stepping out of his old ute that morning, he brought a breath of fresh air and some much-needed mellowness to our build site, even before he enveloped me in a big Kramer bear hug.

We ticked four tricky things off my 'before I move in' list that day.

First, Kramer cut a hole in the laminated bench top for my second-hand kitchen sink. He took a circular saw to my beautiful timber bench – I had to look away – to make a hole for my gas stove. Then he and Max installed the blue bathroom door, a task that required much precision grunting.

After lunch, we all tackled the fourth and final job: 'hanging' the front door. Who knew putting in a door could be so complicated? And this one was heavy (it was made of hardwood and toughened glass like my windows, for safety in transit) and had to open *outwards* like a caravan door, instead of inwards like a regular front door. At one point I left the two of them to wrestle it into position – while one of them held it steady, red-faced and sweating from the awkward weight of it, the other screwed in the last of the four hinges – so that I could finish painting the timber boxes for the downlights in my kitchen.

Half an hour later, everything went quiet. The men-at-work noises had stopped. I put down my paintbrush and stepped out of the garage to check all was OK – and saw that my tiny house finally had a front door. Max didn't hang around to celebrate, but Kramer gave me another hug and I had a little cry. Not just because we were now at the fabled lock-up stage, a milestone on any build, but because the closer we came to finishing the build, the further away Max seemed to be.

That morning we'd seen each other at the beach, by chance, having both pulled up at the same parking area, one of many dotted along the main road of our little town.

'Coming in?' I'd said, stepping out of my car and grabbing my towel, hoping we could have a swim together. Or he could grab his surfboard and catch a few waves while I bodysurfed. No pressure.

'Nup, gonna check the waves up the beach,' he said, suddenly reversing out and driving away. Surfers often check the conditions at multiple spots before paddling out; I've done it myself. And I understood he might have wanted some time alone, or just away from me. But I couldn't help feeling we'd missed another opportunity to do something fun together, to step out of the roles we'd both been playing in the movie of our breakup, to just be two humans in the sea.

After the list-ticking day came a rainy exhale of a day. Max had told me earlier that week that he didn't want to work with me anymore, but working near each other was unavoidable. While rain bucketed down outside, I oiled the high merbau shelf above the timber bench and he put more silicone around the edges of the kitchen sink; while I screwed the downlight boxes to the kitchen ceiling, he gap-filled around the edges. We stepped around each other in the tiny in a silent, awkward dance, the way we had in our first tiny house sleepover, in Edmond. It had been fun then. Which gave me an idea.

I put down the impact driver. 'Want to try something?'

'OK,' he said, sounding wary but willing.

I'd heard about laughter clubs, laughter yoga classes, laughter therapy, World Laughter Day – and how even fake laughing can fool your brain and your body into feeling happier. I told Max my idea; he agreed it was worth a try. We both needed a lift.

He placed his caulking gun on the bench. We stood facing each other, barefoot on the hardwood floor, and started ha-ha-ing and ho-ho-ing, feeling silly and stilted. But within seconds, we were cackling and giggling and guffawing and sniggering and all the time watching each other's faces – smiling at each other's smiles – until we were laughing for real, hopping up and down, feeling as light as two clouds. Feeling happy, at the same time, together.

It ended more naturally than it had begun, like a gentle swell lowering us back to earth. I smiled at Max as he reached for his caulking gun.

'Thank you,' he said, smiling back.

The following day, two young plumbers, brothers Bailey and Lachy, came to finish the plumbing. They drilled holes in my kitchen shelves and in the floor under the cabinets for an outfall pipe from my sink. They put in the gas stove and attached a small hot water unit to the rear wall of the tiny. They made another hole in the floor, in the bathroom, for another drain. They lay on their backs under the tiny, without complaint, to attach white plastic pipes to its underbelly.

I wanted running water and hot showers, of course I did, but a small part of me, the part that still dreamed of living in a rustic cabin or a treehouse with holes for windows and a rope ladder for access, baulked at all the utilitarian bits, all those ugly white pipes, being added to my tiny. Until Bailey and Lachy installed what would become one of my favourite features: my outdoor shower, a steampunk creation of copper pipes and brass fittings, with hot and cold taps, which they attached to the steel cladding near the back of the tiny.

Then came one of the most physically demanding jobs of the build so far, for me at least: digging a ditch between Max's house and the tiny, for my power and water connection. (This was a temporary arrangement; I would disconnect the tiny from Max's house when I moved it to a new location.)

It felt surprisingly good to do some old-fashioned physical labour.

I attacked the ground with a pick, used a spade to cut a channel in the rain-softened earth, clawed at the ground with my gloved hands. It was hot. It rained. Max appeared periodically to tell me to make the ditch deeper and wider. I lost track of time. At one point, I found myself back where I'd been on the very first, very messy day of the build: crawling under the trailer on my belly, in my builders' overalls, my elbows in the mud and gravel. I remembered how happy I'd felt back then, just to be starting the build, blissfully unaware of what lay ahead. Now I was nearing the end of it and feeling happy in a different, fuller way, after all that had happened.

With the power and water conduits in place, I filled in the ditch. And started digging another – for greywater from my kitchen sink, indoor shower and bathroom basin, which would drain into Max's garden.

It was three days of hearty, dirty, satisfying work. And at the end of it, I had my utilities sorted. Whether I was ready or not, the tiny was ready for me.

Chapter 34

# Simple Sundays

There was something I liked to do, to bring myself back to zero when I felt swept away or tossed around by life, a habit that grew into a practice. On idle Sunday afternoons I'd take myself to a nearby headland, find a quiet spot with a wide view of the sea, and spread a cotton blanket on the grass in the shade of a knobbly pandanus palm.

I'd kick off my shoes or sandals and let my bare feet breathe in the earth. I'd look as far as I could. I'd open my ears, find sounds to listen to: a wave breaking, a squeaky-wheel wattlebird in a banksia tree, the wind fluttering the pages of the notebook I'd brought with me. Sometimes I'd write a few words, sometimes I'd fill a page, not to translate the wildness going on around me but to help me pay attention. Mostly I just waited for the thoughts and feelings trailing behind me to catch up and settle down.

Often there'd be dolphins close to shore, in the see-through waves below. All grace and agency, they'd coax me out of my head and hint at another way of being. *See how simple life can be?*

But no two Sundays were alike, even when I returned to the same spot. The sea could be smooth and languid, or salted with white caps. In winter I'd see whales breathing their way north, or gannets whose wingtips would skim the rims of breaking waves beneath my sit-spot. Meanwhile, just beyond my toes, paper daisies might nod in time to the gusts of wind that played with my hair and threatened to run off with my hat. And I always brought my own weather systems. Watching the feelings come and go, like the waves smashing into the rocks and retreating, reminded me they were natural forces, too.

Those afternoons saved me, soothed me, so many times. No matter what was going on inside when I got there, I'd always leave feeling lighter, and more grounded. And the closer I got to moving into the tiny, the more I relied on them. The build, and all the dramas with Max, had swallowed me whole. On top of that, I was in the in-between. My old life, before the pandemic, seemed like something I'd read about once, while the new life I'd been seeking and imagining teased me from up ahead, just out of reach.

But on those Sunday afternoons I could forget all that. I could step out of time, into another space where there was no me, no Max, no build, nothing to plan or understand, no lessons to learn, nothing to let go of. For an hour or two I could be like any other living creature, tuned into an innate and silent knowing that couldn't be put into words, that this was enough, this being alive, this being in the world.

# PART 4
# **LIVING**

*'He who would travel happily must travel light.'*
~ Antoine de Saint-Exupery

## Chapter 35

# If you own a rug

Before every overseas trip, I used to have this recurring dream, no matter where I was going or how long I planned to be away. *Stepping out of a taxi at a big international airport, I suddenly realise – how could this have happened? – I've forgotten all my luggage. Or my passport. I can't miss my flight, my livelihood depends on it, so I hail another taxi, which speeds through peak hour traffic, depositing me at the ferry terminal where I leap aboard, seconds before the gangway is pulled up. On the far side of the harbour, I sprint to my house, turning my departure into a maths problem on the way: if check-in closes at nine, it's seven now and it takes an hour and a half to get back to the airport... Then I'm in the terminal again, skidding across polished floors, weaving between people, shouting for the airport staff at the gate to* please *hold the doors...*

I'd wake up in a nervy sweat every time, believing for several long seconds that I really was late for a flight. *What was I still doing in bed?!*

The same thing happened as I approached my official move-in date. I kept dreaming that some essential part of the tiny had been overlooked during the build. The roof, say, or all the walls. I'd wake up in my rented flat with a jolt and I'd have to talk myself down off the ledge, remind my anxious unconscious that we *had* put the roof on (*remember the celebratory kombucha?*) and built *all* the walls (*those endless nail-punching days?*) and although the little house wasn't finished, it was perfectly safe and liveable.

Every gain involves a loss of some kind and as I packed my worldly possessions into boxes and plastic tubs, I started thinking about the things I'd miss when I left the studio flat I'd called home for six years. Like walking barefoot on the polished concrete floor on hot summer days, and taking long baths on winter nights. How peaceful it was, day and night, because it was away from the street, in the backyard of an old house. Popping next door for a cup of tea with my lovely neighbours, knowing I was always welcome.

One morning I untied from the rafters of my back porch a shell-and-coral mobile I'd made years ago on an island off the Northern Territory's north coast. I'd been there to report on a trip that involved helping the Yolngu rangers remove 'ghost nets' (abandoned fishing nets that endanger turtles and other marine animals) from the island's beaches, in the mornings anyway; in the afternoons my fellow volunteers and I would sit out the Top End heat in a lean-to open to the sea breeze, with our toes in the sand, talking and making things. (The sea was, unfortunately, off-limits because of the saltwater crocodiles.) On one of those afternoons we threaded small chunks of coral, sun-bleached shells and crooked fingers of driftwood onto lengths of fishing line, making our own souvenirs to take home. I took mine back to Sydney, then up the coast when I moved north, but there was no place for it in my tiny and it had been gradually disintegrating anyway. So, like a reverse-craft project, I dismantled it, untying all the knots, disposing of the fishing line and putting all the shells and the pieces of coral and driftwood in a paper bag.

At my local beach just before the move, I emptied the bag onto the wet sand, within easy reach of the waves. Almost immediately, a tablecloth of whitewater spread itself over the shells and bits of coral and pieces of wood and carried them back towards the sea in a single gulp, leaving no trace they were ever there. It felt like a symbolic letting go to match the bigger, more internal one that was happening. Letting go of stuff, letting go of another home, letting go of Max. Like standing on the edge of a cliff, looking out across an expanse of clear sky at something new that I could feel was coming, but couldn't quite make out yet.

After that, I started feeling excited again about what I was moving *to* – my beautiful bright, unfinished, little house that was all wood and windows, lumber and light – and counted down the sleeps until moving day.

A few days before I had to leave my old flat, Max helped me load up his van with boxes, bags, plastic tubs, backpacks, camping gear and my two surfboards.

'Sure you've got enough stuff?' he teased, lugging yet another heavy book box up the steps and into the van. Seeing it all in one place like this, I had to agree. I did have too much stuff.

'If you own a rug, you own too much,' Jack Kerouac once, allegedly, said. I owned a rug and I definitely owned too much. Much more than the laptop, surfboard and duffel bag full of clothes I'd arrived on the north coast with, six years earlier. I'd been a rolling stone on my travel sabbatical, but as soon as I'd stopped rolling, I'd started gathering stuff. New stuff, used stuff, found stuff. Stuff people gave me. Stuff I inherited when Dad moved house. Old stuff I'd retrieved from a storage unit I'd had in Sydney – more books, more clothes, a guitar I'd had since I was twelve, things with question-marks hovering over them. *Would I need this one day? Did I still fit into that? Why, for the love of God, did I still have this?* Enough stuff to counter all my minimalist intentions.

Moving was a chance to correct this. So as I packed, I decluttered. I might not have been doing the classic downsize from a regular house into a tiny; my studio, which I'd rented furnished, wasn't much bigger than my tiny. But I wanted to have *less stuff*.

It wasn't the first time I'd attempted to rid my life of extraneous things. My last big move before this had been out of an old red-brick house overlooking Sydney harbour, that share house I'd lived in for ten years. It was the longest I'd lived anywhere since I was ten years old. I loved that harbour house with its bay-window views and its hideous floral carpet, the enormous backyard and the modest rent that didn't even try to keep up with inflation, thanks to our kind-hearted landlords. I lived there with a wonderful menagerie of housemates over the years – musicians, chess players, teachers, botanists, nurses, chefs – until the house was sold and it was just me and all the unwanted couches, coffee tables, vases and saucepans everyone else had left behind.

The big stuff had been easy. As I gave away or sold things for almost nothing, I felt a marvellous, queenly sense of benevolence. The small stuff was harder, mostly because it was all mine. It's only when you have to eyeball each and every thing you own – and decide its fate – that you truly realise how much stuff you have. *How much did I love that stone Buddha that had been sitting ignored on our back patio for years, the fairy lights I'd bought in a night market in Cambodia, those pebbles I'd collected on a beach whose name I'd forgotten?* Sorting through it all was like replaying cherished clips from my life, sometimes in slo-mo (as I sat on that floral carpet weeping over love letters from old boyfriends at two in the morning).

Disposing of my desk in that Sydney house had been the point of no return. I'd made it out of a hardwood door – technically, this had been my first woodworking project – sanding it by hand and slapping on a few coats of varnish before resting it on four milk crates in my room. I was freshly back from living in Japan and figured that working in a kneeling position would be better for my back than sitting in a chair (and it was, until my knees complained and I raised the desk and reluctantly bought an office chair). Amid the constant uncertainty of my life back then, that desk had given me a hint of stability. When I put it on the kerb with a 'FREE' sign taped to it, I almost cried.

I didn't know it at the time, but closing the door on that house marked the embryonic start of my tiny house journey. It's strange how life works; how can any of us know what lies ahead when we close one door and haven't yet found another one to open? Now here I was, about to make another leap of faith into my new, hopefully forever, home.

At least this time I hadn't inherited anyone else's stuff.

But I did have to make everything I owned fit inside the smallest home I'd ever had, its 25 square metres including the space already claimed by my queen bed, the kitchen cabinets and the soon-to-be-built-in stairs and couch (although thankfully these last two would have some built-in storage).

I gave away anything I hadn't used or worn in a while or that didn't spark joy (I'd read all Marie Kondo's books). I spent a wet Sunday culling photos and slides, travel guides and notebooks. Then I unearthed my nemesis: the plastic tub containing all the diaries I'd been keeping since I was twelve (most of them written before we started calling them journals). A tub heavy with angst and glory. Or so I imagined; I hadn't re-read more than a few snippets over the years. Every now and then, I toyed with the idea of making a bonfire of all these words, to rid myself of the past and who I used to be. I always changed my mind before I could find a box of matches, and a few years before the pandemic, I was glad I did.

I'd just returned from Berlin and was working on a travel story about the city for the twenty-fifth anniversary of the fall of the Berlin Wall. For perspective, I re-read my travel diary from 1989 when, as a young backpacker travelling across Europe, I did a day trip to East Berlin, a few uneasy months before the Wall came down.

I wasn't even an aspiring travel writer then. Just a curious tourist recording, for no one but myself, random thoughts and facts such as: at Checkpoint Charlie I had to pass through four electric-locked doors, pay five deutschmarks for a visa and change twenty-five deutschmarks into East German marks as spending money. 'Deserted streets. Old cars. Barbed wire,' I blandly wrote in my diary that night, safely back in West Berlin. I also wrote about meeting a young guide in a museum I visited, who told me he'd never been to West Berlin, though his girlfriend lived there, and that the Tiananmen Square massacre in Beijing the week before had deeply affected him. Three months later, in November 1989, the East German government ordered its guards to open the border.

It was while rummaging through the tub of diaries that I found a slim red notebook I didn't recognise: Mum's travel diary, from 1956. I flipped through it – hearing her voice as I read her handwritten words – and discovered that she'd visited Berlin five years *before* the Wall went up. She and her female travel buddies had been on a bus tour of the undivided city and had passed under the Brandenburg Gate, which had been closed when I went to Germany in 1989. She described Berlin as 'a most beautiful city... with wide, tree-lined streets, autumn colours glorious, and pucker [great] cafes'. It was like talking with her again, both of us sharing our memories of the same city, at the same age, across time. She'd been gone from my life for almost twenty years by then.

I ended up including excerpts from both our diaries in my Berlin story. And despite my minimalist leanings and the fact that I had no idea where, or how, I was going to fit all my diaries in the tiny, I knew I had to keep them.

Chapter 36

# Hammer and kettle

Moving day arrived, cloaked in heavy rain. I drove back and forth between my old home and my new one, dodging squalls, scurrying from car to door, loaded up with boxes and tubs and cushions, trying not to slip or trip on the ramp – still made of two wooden planks and an oil drum – outside the front door of the tiny.

Max and I had talked briefly when I'd arrived with my first load; I'd run up to his house between showers to say hello. He wanted to talk about us, he said, go over everything, once and for all. *Today?* I wanted to talk, too, but this was not the day for that.

'I can't talk today, babe,' I said, preparing to dash out into the rain again and return to the job of moving house. Besides, we'd tried to talk about all this, so many times. It never went well, never changed anything. *Why would today be any different?* In any case, I told him, I wanted us to look forward, focus on what we could do *now*, not on what we'd both said or done in the past. He didn't agree.

'I've just spent six months building you a tiny house!' he said.

It was another slap in the face. I would always be grateful to him for all his hard work and ideas, everything he'd done on the build, but I was tired of everything I'd done being overlooked and undervalued.

I took a deep breath. 'Don't ever say that to me again.'

He turned away. And stayed away. I hadn't expected him to help me that day, but it wasn't the most auspicious start to us living next door to each other.

Despite the pouring rain, the move went well. Friends came over to lend a hand. Katie gave me a bunch of flowers. Jodi brought champagne. Late in the day, I was just about to reply to Jacqui, who lived up the road and had invited me to join her family for dinner, when Max poked his head in the door.

'Want something to eat?' he asked, friendly again. I was a sucker for a peace offering. I declined Jacqui's offer and followed Max up the soggy path to his house. We were both too tired to talk. Instead, plates balanced on our knees in front of the television, we watched a movie in companionable silence.

When the credits started to roll, I stood up and stretched, and we said goodnight. There might have been a hug, I can't remember. I was too exhausted, and too excited about sleeping in my new bed, alone, in my new house.

It had stopped raining. Guided by the torch on my phone, I traced the twisting garden path from Max's house to mine. A minute later, I was opening my front door.

'Hello, little house,' I said. Inside, it still looked and smelled like a building site, albeit one with too many tubs and boxes stacked against the walls. I closed the door behind me, heard the satisfying click.

After brushing my teeth, I climbed the builder's ladder to my bed loft. I'd done this countless times during the build, but now it was dark and I was holding my phone-torch in one hand and a book in the other, and there was a bed up there, an oasis of pillows and a duvet above the chaos downstairs. I crawled under the covers and read a little by torchlight, as if it were any other night, to calm myself so I could fall asleep, though my body was more than ready to rest. I couldn't help pausing at the bottom of each page to look up in wonder at where I was: sitting up in bed in my little house, at last. And as I turned off the torch, it started raining again.

When I woke the next morning – at first light, because I didn't have any curtains yet – I thought: *That was the best sleep I've ever had.* I hadn't stirred all night. Or needed to pee, which was a relief because a trip to the bathroom would have required negotiating the ladder in the dark – and the bathroom had no actual toilet, because I hadn't made it yet. That was one pre-moving job I *hadn't* managed to tick off. (In the meantime, I had a temporary pee-bucket with a lid, and I could use the toilet in Max's house.)

I lay in bed listening to the birds and the rain tap-dancing on the roof just above my head, and watching clouds race across the window-shaped piece of sky I could see. Perfect conditions for snuggling with one's special person in bed.

Right on cue, I heard a knock at the door. I sat up, peered over the edge of the loft and saw Max standing downstairs (in my excitement the previous night, I'd forgotten to lock the front door). He was holding a basket of fresh produce from his garden: avocados, bananas, a pumpkin, some passionfruit, a pineapple. Best housewarming present ever.

'Oh, thank you! That all looks amazing. Want to come up?'

He left the basket on my timber bench, clambered up the ladder and dived under the covers. We lay close, side by side, both in our PJs, listening to the now-pouring rain and looking around us: at the poplar ply ceiling, our cedar feature wall in the other loft, all the awning windows letting in (as I'd hoped) plenty of fresh air but no rain. A year ago all this had been in our heads and on graph paper. Now we were lying in my bed, on the other side of everything, inside this little house we'd built together – were still, technically, building together.

'I'm really happy for you, babe,' Max said. 'And I'm happy you're living here.'

It was such a relief to hear him say that. We snuggled some more.

When the rain eased, we climbed down the ladder and, with my kitchen not yet ready for guests, he invited me over to his place for pancakes.

'I hope things will be smoother for us from now on,' he said as we walked back to his house.

'I hope so, too, babe.' The most stressful parts of the build were behind us. We could take our time with the rest. And maybe living there was going to be OK, after all.

That day felt like a fresh start. We talked and listened to each other more easily than we had in ages, sharing observations, acknowledging each other's feelings; it was as if we'd flicked a switch. I told him how much I loved talking like this, feeling like we were on the same side. He admitted that sometimes he wasn't very good at saying what he meant. I glowed inside. *If it could be like this even some of the time...*

After the pancakes, I spent all day in the tiny, content just to potter and unpack. Every little thing felt absurdly momentous. First cup of tea, while sitting at my bench looking at the trees. First afternoon nap in my day loft (which began as the first time I'd read a book up there, until I nodded off). *Second* time I'd switched on all the lights. That evening, I took advantage of a pause in the rain to step outside. Everything was still an almighty mess inside, but standing in the driveway looking at my little house with most of its lights on and dusk descending, with its cedar cladding and the tall eucalypts behind it, suspended between earth and sky, it looked sublimely simple and serene.

By Monday morning, after moving in on Saturday, we were back on the tools, almost as if nothing had changed. But something had changed, of course: I was now living on-site, inside the thing we were still building. So alongside the hammers and impact drivers, the boxes of nails and tape measures we'd been using for months, were all my personal belongings and household items like my kettle and my clothes, my toaster and my toothbrush. My long timber bench – I ran my hands along it every time I walked past – was a calamity of groceries and screwdrivers, chopping boards and caulking guns.

While the wet season kept living up to its name, Max and I ticked off a few small jobs, one after another. We worked together easily that day. Sticking acrylic angles on the corners of the shower cubicle walls, finishing the merbau sill at the entrance to the bathroom, making a start on my timber-slat bed base. When the rain held its breath for a few minutes, we carried my oven from the garage into the tiny and plugged it in.

That first week was like a litmus test, for me and for the tiny, as we got to know each other in a new way. One of the first things I noticed, on those first rainy days, was that my new home was wonderfully cosy, without feeling cramped or stuffy – and incredibly spacious. I almost couldn't believe I was now *using* all the features I'd obsessed over for so long. I kept looking around and seeing all the decisions and doubts, all the life lessons and the long days, all the people who had come aboard at various stages to help out, built into every one of them.

It wasn't even finished and already I didn't just love my little house, I loved *being in it*, more than I'd expected to.

I started a mental list of all the bits I loved. It was a long list. There was the silky-smooth timber bench with its rustic butterfly joints. The gas-strut window that brought the trees and the breeze and the bird calls inside with one gentle shove on its frame. The outdoor shower, and the being naked outside, in a driveway on a suburban street, discreetly out of view. The little alcove above my bench, with the 'welcome home' rock Max had given me and a few of my latest found objects, including a pheasant feather and some cowrie shells. I loved feeling the hardwood floor under my bare feet. And that climbing the builder's ladder to my bed loft – until my stairs were built – felt like sneaking up to my own private eyrie.

Unfamiliar with using a galley kitchen, I made myself dizzy at first turning from one bench to the other and back again – until I learned *not* to keep turning in the same direction – but I'd never had so much bench space. And I loved the plain and simple look of my food jars lined up on the kitchen shelves, along with a few books (I seemed to have more kitchen shelving than I needed, and more books than I remembered).

I loved that I could check the weather as soon as I woke up every morning, without even getting out of bed. I noticed where the sun was rising this time of year. With so many windows, and so many of them open at any one time, I could sense the slightest shift in wind direction and how the temperature changed throughout the day. I knew the instant it started raining, and the moment it stopped. On clear nights, I'd lie on my side to watch the stars before I fell asleep. Sometimes the moon would wake me like a sudden spotlight as it rose over the tops of the trees to the east.

And underneath all this house love was a quiet feeling of satisfaction, not quite ready to stand up and be proud, not yet – there was still a lot to do – but beginning to unfurl all the same.

I was still short of places to sit; all I had was my office chair and a couple of milk crates. I was looking forward to having a working toilet. And for my first few days – until I rigged up a makeshift curtain on the large window facing the street – I felt like a live model in a shop window, particularly after dark. All through the build, the tiny had attracted a steady stream of interested friends and curious strangers and I'd loved showing people my little house, but moving in had added a new variable: its human inhabitant. Because the tiny had been designed *for me*, I'd deliberated over every detail and everything was almost finished, it felt as if I was 'on show' now, too. The way I am, the way I live, the way I want to live, the person I want to be. All my preferences were in full view. And I wasn't just the owner, but the designer and the co-builder as well. The tiny house *was* me.

I knew it was premature, and I didn't want to jinx this, but by the end of that first week I felt as if the tiny had passed a crucial test. Everything we'd made so far… worked. The little house felt safe, comfortable and structurally sound. And for the first time in my life, I owned the home I lived in. As milestones go, this was a big one, though it arrived without fanfare, the way a small boat might putter to a safe anchorage it hadn't quite believed it would ever reach, after a long and difficult voyage.

Chapter 37

# Going it alone

After I moved into the tiny, the air between Max and me became warmer and stiller. We were working together without arguing, even playing together. There was friendly banter, there were morning cuddles in my loft, we went surfing together a couple of times. I didn't think: *How long will this last?* I thought: *See, we can do this.*

One day, I made us lunch – I was still getting used to using my new kitchen – and we ate together in the day loft and fell asleep afterwards like a couple of cats, surrounded by cushions. That night, we had dinner at his place. He played his guitar and we sang together for the first time in months, our voices entwining like they used to, and I was surprised at how strong and self-assured mine sounded.

Something had shifted in me with the move, or was in the process of shifting. More than any other move I'd done, this one felt like the turning of a page, as if my outer circumstances were finally aligning with who I was inside; maybe that explained the sense of calm I felt in those first weeks. My little house might have been on wheels, but it made me feel settled. And it was a tangible bit of *me*, right in Max's driveway, impossible to ignore, encouraging the rest of me to stand taller and feel comfortable taking up space.

Later that week, I had a session with Sean. As I was telling him how things were with Max, that it didn't feel like we'd broken up, I realised something: after being so intensely central to my life and my sense of who I was for so long, this relationship was peripheral to me now, to what was happening to me. I'd stopped orbiting Max and judging myself by his criteria. I was feeling happier, learning to trust my intuition again and listening to my body about what was and wasn't true.

Sean had been one of my staunchest allies since I'd started my individual sessions with him. He wasn't on my side just because he was my therapist, but because he'd seen the way Max and I interacted. That had been immensely healing. And helped me see, while I sat in one of his comfy armchairs that day, that maybe choosing to stay with Max *hadn't* been the right thing.

Maybe the right thing, the healing thing, *wasn't* always to find someone you loved and stick with them no matter what, learning whatever life lessons the relationship could teach you. I'd been seduced by an idea that had seemed sound: when emotional wounds come from relationships, healing happens in relationship. It had taken me all this time to realise it had to be the *right* relationship. There had to be trust and constancy, mutual sharing, a sense of emotional safety. The love Max and I had felt, still felt, for each other had tricked me into thinking that being with him would heal my wounds when, too often, it had inflamed them.

When I finished saying all this to Sean, he smiled. 'You're in transition,' he said, our time almost up. He was right, on so many levels. It felt so familiar, so normal to me, this being in limbo, I almost hadn't noticed. I was so used to believing that life was just like this, a perpetual motion picture show that carried us along with it, I hadn't stopped to think it could be any other way. Maybe it could be another way.

A new story might have been unfolding, but Max and I were still reading from an old playbook: things were good between us, until they weren't. The week after I moved in, we found ourselves in the tiny having another argument.

'You can finish the build yourself!' he said, slamming my gas-strut window on his way out.

That night, after an early dinner, I carried Max's words up to my bed loft and curled up with them under the covers. *Just let them be, let them change*, I thought. And they did change, into relief. Without Max's help, I realised, the build would undoubtedly take longer to finish, but there'd be no more misunderstandings, no more dramas or emotional roadblocks.

Maybe this was the opportunity I'd been waiting for. I'd been planning to do more of the work myself anyway, now that we were ready to tackle the built-ins. I could ask others for help. I had some skills. I could make things. Could I make a bed base, a couch, a desk, a ladder and a compost toilet? I was about to find out.

## Chapter 38

# Stairs and strangers

After his decision not to work on the tiny anymore, Max didn't speak to me for three days. I left him alone. And tried to keep my head down, keep working.

Then the stairs arrived.

A couple of months earlier, I'd had to make a big decision. I'd already designed the stairs to my bed loft, puzzled over their 'risers' and 'goings' (the vertical height and horizontal depth of each step), tailored their measurements to my own (my height, for instance, so I could stand fully upright on the top step), figured out the storage configuration underneath. I'd watched videos of home-builders making tiny house stairs. But even back then, building the stairs with Max seemed impossible, and they were way too complicated for me to attempt on my own. This mountain was too high for me.

I was on track financially, sort of, but I was worried that commissioning someone to make the stairs would blow out my budget for the interior. Not only that, but hiring a professional felt like cheating on a DIY build, particularly for such a vital part of my tiny. *Wasn't this all part of the journey, figuring things out when they got tough?*

But things were beyond tough by then. So I walked around the mountain and paid Sam, a furniture-maker recommended by a friend, to climb it for me.

It was early April, the day before the Easter long weekend, pouring rain – I was starting to see 'bad' weather as a good omen – when Sam backed his truck up the driveway. He and his two apprentices unloaded the stairs in boxy sections, along with an assortment of drawers, cupboard doors and treads, then got to work assembling all the pieces and screwing the finished stairs to the wall opposite my timber bench.

Ninety minutes later, I climbed actual stairs to my bed loft for the first time. Made of fawn-coloured birch ply to match my poplar ply ceiling, they were gorgeously simple, all clean shapes and artful 'shadow-lines' (Sam's idea) that made each tread seem to float above the staircase itself.

As soon as Sam and his guys left, my stairs made themselves at home, inviting me to unpack some of my things into their nooks and drawers, offering a new way to access my high windows and suggesting new places to sit; perched on one step, the step above happened to be just the right height to rest an elbow or a cup of tea. Installing the stairs also meant I could finally start working on the couch and other built-ins that needed to fit around them.

Order was slowly spreading from one end of the tiny to the other.

There was just one small problem. Sam had left a gap between the top step and the floor of my bed loft. He preferred open staircases, he'd said, but I wanted the stairs to be joined to the loft, to separate the kitchen from the rest of the tiny; in any case, we agreed we'd figure out a solution. I was still thinking about it when Max wandered into the tiny later that morning to look at the new stairs. He saw the gap and instantly suggested that Sam make a slim plywood box to fill the gap, with shelves facing the kitchen area to store cups and glasses. It was a great idea. Sam agreed to make the box and he brought it over a few days later.

But this new birch ply box created a new problem of its own: the back of it, the bit you could see as you climbed the stairs, had visible end-grain (which looks like wafer biscuits) on both sides. Sam said he'd made it that way deliberately, but to me it looked like a mistake, because it didn't match the rest of the staircase. I told him I'd think about it and call him later; maybe I'd get used to it.

After Sam left, Max appeared again.

'Small problem with the box,' I said, before explaining why I wasn't happy with it. I thought Max would agree; he likes things to be finished properly too.

'You mustn't have communicated clearly,' he said. He knew I'd drawn up what I'd wanted, sent Sam my drawings *and* discussed the box with Sam before he'd made it. 'You need to take some responsibility for not getting what you wanted. You're playing the victim again.'

*Were we still doing this?* This wasn't about poor communication, at least not between Sam and me.

'Why can't you back me up on this?' I said. Max seemed to be blaming *me* for Sam not doing what I'd asked. Was it male solidarity? Another way to put me in my place? Was he just uncomfortable with me expressing *any* disappointment, even if it wasn't directed at him? I didn't have any energy to figure this out. I was so tired of him trying to find fault with me or correct me. He kept talking, kept telling me I wasn't being honest with myself.

'Stop,' I said. 'Please. Don't say anything else unless it's supportive.'

He stopped speaking, and left.

I sat on my new staircase, still feeling unsettled, and a solution to the box problem popped into my head: Sam could glue another panel of ply onto the wrong-looking panel, which would hide those unsightly edges.

'No problemo,' Sam said, when I called to tell him my idea. He brought over the new panel the following day. Mission accomplished.

I felt good about standing my ground with Max, but I was annoyed with myself for involving him in my decision-making process again. *Why did I keep doing that?* Was I just hard-wired to keep seeking ways to connect, even when I knew they'd probably backfire?

I was constantly trying to shrink my expectations for our interactions. Trying to see how low they could go. I thought: *I just want to be treated like a stranger.* That was one of the things I missed about travelling: random, kind encounters – on buses, in city streets, at markets, on mountain trails – with people who know nothing about you. All you share is a brief moment when your lives bump up against each other. You smile, they smile back. That simple acknowledgement of our shared humanity could fill me up for days, especially when I travelled alone.

But Max and I were not strangers. And I knew it was unrealistic to expect him to treat me like one. It would have required a temporary forgetting – never mind forgiving – of all that had happened between us, a living in the eternal now.

So I started playing another game in my head: how would we speak to each other if we were friends, if we'd never fallen in love? It seemed a reasonable baseline for common decency. *Would he speak to George that way? How would I say this if Max were my friend, or someone I didn't know?*

But it was hard to sustain even that, in the face of our unrelenting reality that we weren't partners, we weren't strangers, we weren't friends. We were living in a no-man's-land we each had to navigate as best we could, in our own way.

Chapter 39

# Co-working

This is how a build is sometimes: you move in, the house almost finished, the build keeps going. You want it done. You want to move on with your life, think about something other than materials and measurements, change the channel. But you have to keep watching, until the show is over. It wasn't over yet.

After moving into the tiny, I lost my momentum. In gaining a home, I'd lost a deadline. I found myself doing less and procrastinating more. There was a part of me that, having found a comfy nest, really didn't want to put on a toolbelt and get back to work. I tried to cajole it into action with chocolate fudge and a few days off.

I kept going.

In one sense, moving in before my little house was finished had felt like a second-best outcome, but it had one big advantage: the tiny could show me how to live in her (somehow, quite suddenly, she'd also gained a gendered pronoun). By doing everyday things like washing the dishes and putting away my clothes, noticing how I used the space and how I wanted to, I was learning firsthand how to make the last things. She was guiding my final decisions about how long the couch should be, how wide the desk needed to be, where the ladder to the day loft could go…

Then, just as I was preparing to tackle all these projects alone, things changed again.

It happened on Max's birthday. He was turning sixty and although he didn't like parties or dining out, I wanted to set aside our problems for a day, help him mark the occasion. And he didn't seem to have organised anything with anyone else. So, early that morning, I walked up to his house and gave him a book and a gift voucher for a massage – to help ease the stress of the past seven months – and invited him over to the tiny for breakfast and hot cross buns. He came over, but he wasn't really there. Until, inevitably, we started talking about the build and he fired up with plans and ideas about my ladder and the couch and it was nice and… confusing. *He'd said he was done with the build. Did he want to keep working on it now? Was he just trying to help me?* I knew how this went: confusion too often led to misunderstandings, which led to disconnection. So I suggested we take a break from talking about the tiny; he went home.

I drove to the lake for a swim and sat under the trees and let my senses lead me back to what was real, what I could trust. *I'm breathing. My hair is dripping down my back. The dappled shade of the paperbarks. The sun. My skin feeling cool and shivery from the wind. Water, a streaky sky, an osprey.*

Back home, feeling grounded again, I took some picnic supplies up to Max's house, the last part of his birthday present. He was quieter, too, gave me a hug, invited me to share the picnic with him.

'I'll help finish the build,' he said, pouring us some tea. 'But I want to work alone.'

That explained why he'd been brimming with ideas that morning. I knew that with his help, everything would be finished sooner than if I worked alone, but I didn't want any more surprises. And I didn't want him to take over, to finish everything himself. This was still my project, my home, my adventure.

'How about we work alone, together?' I said, not really sure what this might mean in practice.

'Deal,' he said, spreading a picnic rug on the daybed on his verandah.

After we'd eaten our fill of cheeses, dips and fresh crusty bread, we lay side by side. My heart slowed. I felt sleepy. It always surprised me, the way my body rattled and purred around him, depending on what was happening between us, the energetic pulse that was always there.

'It's such a shame we can't get along,' he said, turning onto his side and draping one arm over me.

'Yeah,' I said, moving closer. I still couldn't resist these moments of connection, even if there was no promise in them. Maybe because there wasn't, because that was liberating. I could just enjoy Max's company, safe in the knowledge that this wasn't my final destination, because I was starting to see what that looked like now. It looked like freedom *and* stability, not one at the expense of the other.

We stuck to the new plan. All that month, Max and I worked alone, together, making the built-in furniture for my tiny.

Sometimes he did his own thing. He made the frame and the plywood base for my couch, for instance, even added a couple of second-hand seat cushions and placed them on top with a few smaller pillows from his own house when he'd finished, to show me how it would all look. Sometimes I did my own thing, too. I made a pine shelf for my bathroom. I bought two birch stools from IKEA and, finding them too high for my timber bench, sawed 50 millimetres off the bottom of each leg before sanding the seats of both stools to colour-match them to my birch-ply stairs. After reading the surprisingly fascinating bible of composting, *The Humanure Handbook* by Joseph Jenkins, I made my compost toilet, which turned out to be easier, and more fun, than expected and involved more than a bit of (fully clothed) pretend-peeing over a wooden box in the garage.

Sometimes we worked alone *and* together, each of us making different parts of the same thing. For my day-loft ladder, I measured and designed it, Max cut and assembled all the bits, and I sanded and coated the finished product. When Max shaped a beautiful handrail for my stairs from a strip of white gum (an offcut from my timber bench), it was my job to sand it smooth all over. One morning in the garage, I propped it up on two sawhorses, sat astride it and started rubbing its long shaft with a piece of sandpaper between my fingers, working up a sweat, totally absorbed in what I was doing, unaware of how this might have looked – until Max, walking past, stopped to watch.

'Ooh, er,' he said, raising his eyebrows.

'Yeah, baby,' I replied, caressing the long length of wood with my sawdusty hands. It felt good to be silly together.

Another day, Max asked me to buy a 'round bastard' at Bunnings. I wasn't completely sure he wasn't pulling my leg, but when I arrived at the store I discovered an entire section devoted to 'bastards' of all kinds (steel files of various shapes and sizes). The round bastard I was looking for – a cylindrical file, with a handle, used for smoothing out the insides of holes – was right next to the half-round bastard, the triangular bastard, the flat bastard and, my favourite, the general purpose bastard. I had a smile on my face all the way home.

We decided to make the last built-in, the desk, together. The first part was pretty straightforward: basically remodelling a desk Max had made for me when I was living in my rented studio. After he removed the four legs and cut the desk to the right length, I took to it with a belt sander, stripping away its dark stain to reveal a patchwork of lighter strips of acacia. It looked like a quilt made of reindeer pelts, which suited the accidentally Scandinavian decor in the rest of the tiny: lots of white, lots of wood, soft grey furnishings. Then I rounded one corner of the desk with a jigsaw to match the rounded end of my timber bench.

Installing the desk was more complicated because it was cantilevered, like the bench, to maximise open space beneath it. So I deferred to Max's superior know-how, let him wear the boss's cap again. It took us *all* day. And all that day we didn't argue. Well, not with each other; Max regularly swore at his tools and pieces of wood that didn't do his bidding and I got used to hearing 'cunt of a thing!' without flinching.

Much as I loved the autonomy of working on my own projects, I loved this, too. It was like a personal woodworking class. And I was a better apprentice than I'd ever been; I knew all the tools we were using, what they did, where they were kept, when we might need them. I didn't ask questions, didn't expect Max to chat with me the way he might have with George, didn't take anything he said personally, just wanted to help get the job done. And he kept his end of our unspoken agreement by not talking down to me or finding fault with what I did. We were master and apprentice, simple as that.

That afternoon, after Max had gone home and I'd cleaned up our worksite, I stood at my new desk under the big north-facing window, looked over at my new couch and up at my new ladder, and inhaled the aroma of sawdust and satisfaction – not just for the things we'd made, but for the way we'd managed to make them.

Chapter 40

# May Day

It was the first of May, our anniversary, in my mind at least. We'd had our picnic on the headland and our first kiss that day, four years earlier, but Max had never liked that date. He hadn't felt ready, he said, didn't think of that as the real start of our relationship. He picked a date in October, instead, when I'd absent-mindedly drawn a love heart on the calendar he kept on his kitchen bench. We'd compromised – decided to have two anniversaries – but for me May Day (overlooking the unhappy coincidence that 'mayday' is an international distress signal) would always mark the start of us. So when it rolled around during the build, I thought we could create a new anniversary from the ashes of the old one.

Early that morning, I padded over to Max's house in my PJs, the sky dawdling from pre-dawn pink to daylight blue. On his verandah, I pressed my nose to his sliding glass door, to see if he was up yet. He was in the kitchen. He waved me inside.

'Cup of tea?' he said, as I slid open the door.

'Yes, please. And Happy Build Anniversary. What do you think? I've moved into the tiny, we've finished all the built-ins. I mean, we still need to tinker and make the deck and a few other things. But it could be our new anti-versary.'

He answered by wrapping me in a long hug and kept holding me close while he switched on the kettle and reached over to the fridge to get some milk, sliding around in his socks as I stood on his feet like a little girl, feeling playful. The kettle boiled and he made the tea and invited me up to his loft. We passed our cups up the ladder to each other and sat on his bed. He suddenly became serious.

'What is it about me, and what I do, that upsets you so much?' he said.

It was too early in the day for such a big question. What could I say that hadn't been said before, in so many ways? I appreciated that he was trying to understand, but it put me on the back foot again. I was unprepared, being asked to explain myself, help him see things he hadn't seen before. It felt like a test: *Why can't we be together? Why did our relationship fail? You've got ten minutes. Your time starts now.* And I didn't want us to fall into the old pattern where all the focus was on me.

At the same time, it was an open door; I didn't want to close it in his face. So we talked, taking turns to share and listen. There was some comfort in both feeling some of the same things: a deep love for each other, a frustration that we were stuck, an ambivalence/uncertainty about where to go next. But the more we talked, the sadder I felt. It suddenly seemed so tragic that there was this great love right in front of us – and just out of reach.

'Come here, beautiful girl.' We put our cups on the window sill, wriggled under the covers and slipped off our PJs. Long exhale. I'd forgotten how good this felt.

'I miss sleeping with you,' I whispered.

'Me too. I love you, Loui.'

'Love you too,' I said.

Holding each other close led to kissing to... feeling sexy and desired and forgetting all the trying and the wanting to understand and be loving and loved and good, and we broke the cardinal rule of breaking-up (again). And it was easy and beautiful and free, our physical connection the clearest and best thing about us, still, the wonder of it.

A few days later, I walked past the garage while Max was cutting a length of copper pipe. The angle grinder was noisy and violent so I kept my distance, but I stopped to watch the spark shower it made every time he touched it to the metal pipe.

When he'd finished what he was doing, Max removed his earmuffs and safety glasses and came over to me. Handed me a shiny, rough-edged copper ring.

'Will you marry me?'

'Maybe,' I said. We both knew he was messing around, but I tried on the ring. It fit snugly on my right ring finger. I hadn't wanted to put it on my left hand, hadn't wanted to play along *that* much. Then I remembered: in some countries, people wear their wedding bands on the right hand.

I rarely wore jewellery – and still never wear rings when I'm working with my hands – but I wore that little copper ring for weeks afterwards. As a reminder of the changeless thing that still flowed between us, just under the surface, under all our struggles and silences, like a snow-covered woodland stream that, if you crouched low and kept very still, you could hear gurgling and swirling, surrendering, continuing.

Chapter 41

# The great slow-down

May became a month of making. Max started on the deck, a modular design that would be easy to take apart when I needed to move the tiny, then disappeared for half the month, on two separate van-camping trips with his friends. I was pleased he was going away, and pleased to be left behind. I wanted some alone time to do some making of my own.

I'd always felt different when he wasn't around, but that difference was amplified now I was living on his land; it was as if I expanded to fill the space he'd vacated – in my head and in my surroundings. The days were smoother, I could work at my own pace, I was more patient with myself. And when doubts came, as they inevitably did, I had the headspace to manage them and talk myself through whatever I was doing.

First, I made some buttons for the open flap at the end of my duvet cover. Four wooden buttons, from offcuts of western red cedar. I could do things like this now. I used a bandsaw to cut four small cedar squares, rounded their corners on a grinder, drilled two holes in each and spent a delightful half-hour sitting in the sun on an upturned milk crate, sanding the buttons by hand.

After all those months of working on the tiny, the simple satisfaction of crafting those four wooden buttons quietly blew my mind.

So I looked around for other small wooden things to make. I made a wooden flower – also from leftover cedar – to cover a hole in the wall above my timber bench where I'd changed my mind about a light fitting. Followed by two more, to decorate my bathroom. More wooden buttons, to replace three old plastic ones on a favourite cushion. A camphor laurel chopping board and a matching wooden bowl, which involved learning how to use a friend's very loud, and quite scary, lathe.

One morning I was chatting with Katie outside her place – her front door faced my tiny – and she showed me her much-loved wicker sewing basket. It had belonged to her grandmother and had a pretty printed lining, but had lost its lid.

'I can make a new lid for you,' I said, before I had any idea how I might do that. I figured out a way: cut a piece of plywood to size, made two finger-holes in the top (simpler than a handle), glued little stopper strips under its edges to keep the lid in place, then coated it in clear sealer. Katie loved it. And I loved that having new skills meant I could make things for other people as well as for myself.

As the nights became cooler, I borrowed a friend's sewing machine and made two curtains for the downstairs windows, for privacy as well as for warmth, another first for me. I put up a mirror, installed the splashbacks around the kitchen sink and bathroom basin, hung a canvas frangipani print on the wall of my kitchen, and painted the ugly white downpipe outside, dark grey to match my steel cladding. I even cleaned and scrubbed Max's garage, to surprise him on his return.

But I was happiest sitting in the sun on that upturned milk crate, sanding a small piece of wood on its way to becoming something useful. I loved the honest simplicity of small woodworking tasks, more than I expected to, the instant feedback that came directly from your hands, telling you how you were doing, when to keep going, when you were done.

Some of the peace of that month undoubtedly came from the fact that the build, this beautiful monster that had dominated my life for the better part of a year, was almost over. I was starting to see glimmers of a life beyond the endless to-do lists, and wondering what it might look like. When I thought about my pre-build life – my mind dashing off in different directions, to different destinations, always seeking story ideas and inspiration, while my body waited patiently at the desk – I felt in no hurry to return to it. I wasn't even in a hurry to travel again. I was still figuring out what I wanted, what was possible, but I didn't want to forget how good and true it felt to work like this, with my mind and my body, for once, in the same place.

⌂

At the end of May, after we'd all made it through the entire build accident-free, except for a few splinters and hammered thumbs, I had a succession of slips and mishaps, bumps and scrapes.

First, I fell off a ladder, just from a low rung but I landed hard on my elbow.

I slipped on a wet paving stone and wrenched my right knee.

My left thigh started aching from crouching to protect my right knee.

I had an awkward fall on the plank-and-drum 'drawbridge' outside my front door, grazing my arm and twisting my wrist.

I got a small ulcer inside my mouth.

One of my toes swelled up for no reason.

And my hands began aching. The pain was faint at first. I'd wake in the morning with sore finger joints. Then my fingers got puffy and my whole right hand swelled up. I went to the doctor, had some blood tests and scans; no medical cause was found. I put it down to eight months of using heavy power tools designed for man-sized hands. And installing the splashbacks in the kitchen earlier that month; the trigger of the silicone caulking gun was so stiff I'd had to squeeze it as hard as I could, with both hands, to get the sticky silicone out of the nozzle. Oh, and emotional stress.

After feeling stronger and more able-bodied than I'd felt in years, I suddenly could not open a jar. I had to use two hands to turn on the gas stove or pull on the handbrake in my car. I stopped surfing because I couldn't push myself up on my surfboard. Holding a power drill or an electric sander was out of the question.

The physiotherapist gave me splints to keep my wrists immobile.

But it wasn't just my hands that needed a rest. My whole body was calling a stop-work meeting. I was, all over and in all ways, spent. And it's harder to argue with the body than with the mind. So I didn't try. I listened, and rested.

June, therefore, passed in a homely fashion, something I was unaccustomed to. The days became shorter and colder. It was the season for hibernating and getting cosy indoors. And my tiny house, I discovered, was a very good place to get cosy.

I baked cookies and cakes and bread, glorious bread. Is there anything in the world more comforting than a small house filled with the heady scent of baking bread? I picked flowers and sprigs of eucalypt leaves and put them in jars of water around the house. I sewed and mended and read and took naps. I walked to friends' houses for cups of tea, and made scones when they visited me. I harvested sweet potatoes and pumpkins from the garden and turned them into soup.

I stopped writing to-do lists. I let whole days unfold.

I developed the cat-like knack of following the sun around the tiny, curling up with a book wherever it looked warm, moving only when the sun moved.

Some afternoons I'd make a pot of tea and just sit at the open gas-strut window, looking at the trunks of the big eucalypts that towered over my house and the plants in my small new garden, marvelling at all the botanical living going on, right outside my door.

All that month, I was falling in love with my new home, and with being *at home.*

I felt the way I had in Japan all those years ago: that I didn't have to strive to be happy. The last jobs of the build could wait. I could let life happen. It made me realise how tightly I'd been holding the reins for the past several months, trying to make sure everything ran smoothly, trying to make good decisions and learn new skills and work hard, trying to understand the emotional story playing out underneath and be kind and take care of myself and keep going…

Meanwhile, out in the world, the pandemic raged on. I got vaccinated and listened to the news reports. It seemed to be happening far away, but borders were still closed, so I was still receiving a wage subsidy and now that I was paying less rent – to Max, to park my tiny on his land (he was a generous landlord) – I felt more grateful than ever for my tiny life, for the privilege of being able to rest.

I needed the quiet and stillness for another reason: to process all that had happened in the year since I'd started drawing those first tentative floor plans. I needed to stop moving forward, planning, making decisions, getting things done. I'd been living in the tiny for almost three months, but it was only during this enforced slow-down that it started to feel, day by day, like where I belonged. I'd loved the adventure of getting here, most of it, but oh my God, it was good to be home.

Chapter 42

# Delusional

Towards the end of my slow-down month, Max finished the deck, the last job he'd agreed to do. We'd been keeping out of each other's way, but I was struggling with the emotional distance between us. The struggle was taking its toll.

The day I finished oiling the deck, I took myself out for the afternoon. I had to do some errands, and I wanted to have lunch with Jodi, who lived about forty minutes away. Mostly I needed some physical distance from Max. We'd had an unpleasant interaction that morning when I'd felt hurt by the way he'd spoken to me, and told him so, but the residue of that had faded by the time I headed home. The drive itself was lovely, all meandering country roads, weatherboard villages and views across dairy farms to the nearby ranges. I even sang to myself; I hadn't done that for a long time. I was better at this now, I thought, at letting emotions rise up and fade away. Maybe it was like training for a long hike: being fitter didn't necessarily mean you never got out of breath, but your recovery times improved.

As I was parking my car next to the tiny, Max walked over.

'How'd you go?' he asked. I told him about my afternoon, feeling surprised the lines of communication were open again so soon.

'Can we talk?' he said.

I felt the wariness return. 'Sure.'

He carried a couple of milk crates over from the garage. We sat down. I waited.

'There's something I want to say, and I don't think you're going to like it,' he said.

'OK.' Being away from him for a few hours had made me feel steadier, ready for anything. I wasn't ready for what came next.

'I think you might be delusional,' he said, point-blank.

'What?' Still buoyant from my lovely afternoon, I almost laughed.

But as his words and his surly attitude settled on me, they brought me back to earth with a thud. And with them came a grim realisation: the only possible way Max could make sense of the fact that I'd felt hurt by things he'd said or done – *that he had hurt me* – was to believe that I saw and heard things that weren't really there. Elissa Bassist writes about this in *Hysterical*: 'Anyone can use the language of mental illness out of context to stop a woman's voice dead in its tracks'. Call a woman 'crazy' and anything she says can be dismissed as emotional, not rational, 'and no one has to listen to her anymore'.

'I'm just concerned about you,' Max said, as if he were standing on the deck of a boat, tossing lifebuoys at me while I floundered in the sea. Except I wasn't floundering. I didn't need his lifebuoys. I'd been trying to tell him, show him: *I'm not drowning! I'm a strong swimmer! Look, it's shallow enough for me to stand!*

'Are you still seeing Sean?' More misdirection: I was the one seeing a therapist. Sean called this 'weaponising therapy'. In that moment I could see that Max genuinely believed he was doing the right thing, being a good person. It was the 'doublethink' of the patriarchy. The whole world is set up, says Anna Funder in *Wifedom*, her brilliant book about George Orwell's wife Eileen, 'to allow men to treat women badly, and still think of themselves as decent people'. (Which is not to say that men, boys and non-binary humans don't also suffer in patriarchal cultures like ours; I know they do.)

But it was personal, too. Max was holding onto his own lifebuoys, to ease his own pain. Hurt people hurt people, often without meaning to.

I didn't know what to say, so I reached out to touch his arm.

He pulled it away, stood up and walked back to his house.

Back inside the tiny, I felt shattered. I had been holding steady while I'd been talking with Max, holding my nerve, but my body was in distress. I knew what to do; this was second nature to me now. I checked my racing heart, the act of counting calming me: a hundred beats per minute, almost twice my resting pulse rate. I was probably awash with adrenaline, cortisol and who knows what else, primed to fight, flee or freeze. I was certainly sweaty; I took off the T-shirt and sweater I'd been wearing and tossed them in the washing basket. I stepped out of my undies and my jeans and stood under the shower outside, looking up through the falling water at the trees. Then I put on some warm clothes and did a few simple chores to settle myself: folded my laundry, washed the dishes, boiled the kettle.

Finally, I took a cup of tea up to the day loft and opened my notebook. I wrote down what had happened and how I was feeling about it. Then I wrote Max a letter.

I apologised for my part in the day's conflicts and told him his words – that one word – had really hurt. I said that I understood he meant well and cared about me, but what he'd said wasn't helpful and I was actually doing OK. And it was too soon for us to be friends. Everything was too raw, we were still too entangled, the words between us carried too much charge. Finally, I told him I loved him and appreciated all he'd done for me. I signed off with 'hand on my heart', a greeting I'd brought back from a trip to Jordan when we were still new to each other, one we'd adopted as a way to say 'I love you' whenever we could see each other but were too far apart to speak.

It took me two drafts to get it right, then I typed up my handwritten letter and emailed it to him. It felt good to write it, to attempt repair. I didn't expect him to reply, didn't want to discuss it with him later, didn't have any confidence that would change anything. I just hoped he'd read it, feel the love in it and maybe see that I was doing my best and I wanted peace.

The next morning Max wandered over while I was eating breakfast outside, in front of the tiny. 'Thank you for your email,' he said. I nodded, waited for him to say something else, but he turned and disappeared into his garage. I heard the radio come on and tools being removed from their cases; he was starting work.

He never mentioned the letter, or his 'delusional' comment, again.

It's hard to pick a moment when you know a relationship is truly over, or has changed so completely you don't recognise it anymore. But for all we'd been through, this incident was a line in the sand for me, did more damage to us than almost anything else in our relationship, and left me with a deep and lasting sadness.

My little house and our relationship had been on parallel, but opposite, tracks for ten months. While one was coming together, the other was falling apart. Now that the tiny was virtually finished it made sense, on some cosmic level, that our relationship would properly find its full stop, too. It had been a few months since we'd officially broken up, but this felt like the real ending, the last safety barrier at the cliff edge. Beyond it, there was empty space.

Sitting outside in the sun that morning, I felt becalmed. And relieved to finally set down the emotional load I'd been carrying; there'd be no more trying to understand, trying to love, trying to know when to give in and when to stand firm, when to hold on and when to let go.

It helped that I'd been progressively disentangling myself from Max so I could see where he ended and I began, so the way he saw things – and saw me – no longer counted for everything. It helped that I'd started spending more time with friends who liked and cared about me in ways that made sense to me.

And it helped that I still had work to do, to finish the tiny.

Chapter 43

# Home-making

Years before the build, before the cabin in Norway, I went surfing up the coast with a friend one weekend, a few hours north of Sydney, where I was still living. It was a glorious early-summer morning and we'd been catching lots of waves, but when I paddled for my last one, something happened. As the breaking wave lifted me, my board nose-dived and I fell, hitting the flat water in front of the wave hard, head first. In that instant, I lost my body. I couldn't move or feel anything from the neck down. I was underwater, unable to do anything to get myself to the surface, holding my breath.

My wetsuit saved me that day; it brought me to the surface, moments before my lungs filled with water. Then my friend slid me onto his longboard and paddled me to the beach and I was airlifted to hospital, where I spent two weeks in the spinal unit feeling shaken but lucky, because there was no permanent damage; I'd only bruised my spinal cord. My body returned to me inch by inch, starting at my fingertips and toes.

It was only when I walked – weakly, gingerly – out of hospital that the real healing began. Therapists of all kinds helped me recover from my injury and the trauma of almost drowning. Meanwhile, at home, my wetsuit saved me again. It had been cut off me, from ankle to neckline, when I'd arrived at emergency, so I decided to mend it, as a way to heal my shattered spirit. I bought some black nylon thread, a sturdy needle and a thimble and, stitch by stitch, I hand-sewed my wetsuit, and my confidence, back together. It was another life lesson I'd forgotten about until the build: doing simple, practical things, like mending and making, isn't just calming; it can also be profoundly healing.

⌂

When my hands stopped aching and the rest of me was ready, I started working on the tiny again, with a lighter attitude than I'd had for most of the build. Max was spending more time away with his friends, which gave me the perfect chance to tackle the last woodworking projects on my own, in my own way.

My go-slow month had been a circuit breaker of sorts. I wanted to be gentle with myself. I wanted to worry less and 'have a go' more – even when I didn't know what I was doing. I wanted to let simple, practical work heal my heart.

I started with a basic pine shelving unit, to go in my day loft, for books and the television I didn't have yet. Then I made a larger shelving unit for my bed loft, a more complicated design with a planter box on top and storage for bed linen below. I made a bedside box – effectively a tiny bedside table – where I could stash a few more books; a little Japanese-style 'soap house' from cedar offcuts for my outdoor shower area, to shield my shampoo bars from the rain; and, just for fun, a cedar box for the back of my bike, to match my cedar-clad house.

I worked carefully and methodically. I wasn't so afraid of mistakes now; I knew what to do if a drill bit snapped off in a piece of wood or a screw broke through where it wasn't supposed to. I still couldn't really think in three dimensions, but I got around that by creating tiny cardboard models of whatever I was making – like crude dollhouse furniture – so I could 'see' how many pieces of wood I'd need, how wide and high they had to be, and how they might fit together.

One morning, I was struggling to hold two panels of wood at right angles to each other so I could screw them together. I'd tried clamps, bracing them with my elbows, leaning them against larger blocks of wood, even standing the panels on the ground and supporting them with my legs. Nothing worked. So I had a tea break, searched YouTube on my sawdusty phone and learned how to make L-shaped jigs out of scrap pieces of wood. I made three; they worked a treat.

I learned patience from the varnish I used to coat a low table I made for my deck – by waiting for each coat to dry, applying multiple coats, having to start all over again when the final coat dried lumpy...

If I had trouble concentrating or started to feel bothered in some way, I tuned in to how I was *feeling* about what I was *doing*. Or I stopped for a cup of tea, as Sophie might have suggested. Sometimes I'd talk myself through what I had to do; speaking, like writing, forced my thoughts to walk in single file so I could hear what they were trying to say. And on days that were a struggle from the get-go, I had no qualms about taking the afternoon off, maybe doing some baking or having a nap – which was so unlike me. It seemed the tiny wasn't done changing me yet.

⌂

When I wasn't woodworking, I practised the gentle art of pottering. I learned how to propagate plants, watching in amazement as a stick in a jar of water developed roots and leaf nubs and (eventually) turned into a baby fiddle leaf fig. I planted seedlings for winter veggies and dug up bright yellow chunks of fresh turmeric and ginger to make tea. I watched bees buzzing between cosmos flowers that grew wild on the footpath in our street; sometimes I'd pick a few of the cosmos to bring their pretty purples and pinks inside. I bought a second-hand sewing machine and made my first cushion cover, followed by some curtain ties and a simple beach dress – all from the same fabric, the way Julie Andrews in *The Sound of Music* made the von Trapp children's frocks and lederhosen, and a dress for herself, from a single printed curtain.

I was home-making in the truest sense of the word.

Sometimes I'd sit in my day loft, looking at everything and reliving scenes from the build – laying the hardwood floor, sanding the ceiling, creating my kitchen, painting the walls – and thinking about how much care had gone into every detail, and I'd fall in love with my little house all over again.

It still amazed me that I was living like this. Me, the commitment-phobic, nomadic, home-is-a-hotel travel writer. Was I still that person? Was I just playing at living simply until Australia's international borders reopened? Or was I making space for another me, the one who had been homesick for twenty years without knowing it, without knowing where home really was or what it could be?

In the tradition of women everywhere since the beginning of time, I felt a bit guilty about having all this unstructured time, as if I was wagging school or dodging a bigger, more selfless life. It seemed indulgent. I tried to see it as a reward for surviving the build and the breakup, this grand adventure that was coming to an end.

Then I wondered if my new, homely lifestyle was anti-feminist. Wasn't this the kind of life women had been struggling to escape for so long, the kind that women of my generation had studied hard to avoid? Girls like me had been groomed from our first nervous days at school for high-achieving lives, not domestic ones (as if these two options were mutually exclusive). My school's motto was even 'Strive for the highest'.

Yet here I was, living a paradox: everything I'd learned from teachers and from travel had ultimately, in a most circuitous way, led me to this simple life. I didn't know if this was me now and forever – if we're ever 'done' figuring out how to live – but I didn't need to know; I was just happy I'd finally found it.

Chapter 44

# Boltholes

In mid-July I did something I hadn't done for two years: I went camping. For three days, alone, down the coast. I'd almost forgotten how to pack, not that I needed to take much. I dragged my camping gear out of the underfloor storage unit in the tiny, stuffed some clothes in a bag, put food in an esky I kept under the trailer. Then I booked a campsite by the beach in a nearby national park and drove south.

For three days, I dawdled along empty beaches, wandered through paperbark forests, ran (again, like Julie Andrews) over grassy headlands. There were frigid early morning swims and starry, rugged-up campfire nights. I spent a lazy afternoon reading and dozing in an orange and lolly-pink hammock I'd bought in Panama years ago. One morning, sitting on a dune near my camp, my hands wrapped around a mug of tea, I watched two kangaroos, backlit by the early sun, slow-hopping up the beach, along the water's edge.

My nervous system relaxed, my stomach knot untied itself. I'd needed this kind of break – uninterrupted, unplugged, unwatched – more than I'd realised. At first, without the usual distractions, I was overcome by a great wave of feelings. I cried on the beach and in the sea and in my tent. Then things settled and I became calmer and more content.

I'd been such a homebody, in every sense of the word, ever since I'd started designing my tiny and imagining the kind of home I wanted, I'd forgotten about the part of me that loves to play and be in nature for longer than an hour or two.

I'd also forgotten that you need to go away to experience the joy of coming home.

It was the first time I'd come home to the tiny. As I drove up the driveway towards my little house late in the afternoon, I felt unexpectedly excited, seeing it again, unlocking the door, breathing in the scent of cedar. It still smelled new inside.

It was good to see Max, too. He walked over from the garage when he'd heard my car. Having barely spoken to another soul for a few days, I was more aware than ever of that electricity I always felt around him – and a carefulness that was a constant for me now whenever I was with him.

'I'm glad you're home,' he said, looking me in the eye. We hugged and he asked about my trip. I told him about the kangaroos, the waves, the stars, feeling a pang under my words. *We could have been there together.* But I found myself not needing his attention. I was fully inhabiting my own skin, all powered-up on nature. I'd emptied out my head. I felt softer – and stronger – than when I'd left.

The peace of that little trip lingered for days like a good-natured shadow. And something occurred to me: for the first time, my home wasn't just a bookmark, a place-holder reminding me where to come back to after I'd done my real living somewhere else. My home and my life were finally happening in the same time zone, the same place, instead of on opposite sides of the world. I'd needed to go away to see that. And travel, that thing I'd always loved but had turned my back on during the build like a bad friend, had found me again and followed me home.

My very last woodworking project was a bench for the small deck Max had made at the front of the tiny, over the trailer drawbar. It started as two lengths of spotted gum – one long, one shorter – which I planned to attach to the top of a low L-shaped railing, as a seat. Like every little job on the build, it was bigger than anticipated and took longer than expected. But I had plenty of time – because we were in lockdown.

It was August and northern NSW, which had escaped the worst of the pandemic until then, finally had its first extended lockdown. It would end up lasting only five weeks, which was nothing compared to the months-long stay-at-home orders people had endured in Melbourne, Sydney and other parts of the world. Still, it meant a period of enforced confinement in my very new, very small house.

I wondered if, under these new circumstances, I'd suddenly find my tiny too small. But it didn't feel confining at all. On the contrary, I liked having the chance to spend more time in it, to explore all its nooks and discover new spots to sit with a cup of tea and a book, without feeling any pressure to be somewhere else. The days slowed down and filled themselves up with solitary indoor activities like mending and reading, bookended by early morning swims and late afternoon walks.

I know it wasn't easy for some, but for me it was a delightfully idle time, punctuated by the slow, careful making of that L-shaped bench seat.

That's when a word caught me by surprise.

It happened after the endless measuring, the cutting, the sanding, the oiling. I was finally ready to bolt the planks onto the railing of my front deck. I drilled holes for the six cup-head bolts I planned to use. Six holes, for six bolts. Six *boltholes*. I rolled the word around in my mouth. It sounded familiar. And as I dropped the last bolt into its hole and hand-tightened the nut underneath, I realised that this little word neatly summed up how much my life had changed over the past year. How much, perhaps, we had all changed.

Once upon a time, I'd written travel stories about 'boltholes' as hideaways from the world, places to escape the stresses of everyday life. Then our homes became boltholes, for better or worse, places to take refuge from the pandemic. Now a 'bolthole' was, to me, nothing more than a hole for a bolt to go through.

This build had taught me so many new words. Now it was bringing a word I already knew back to earth.

Is a home you build yourself ever truly finished? I'd been starting to wonder if mine ever would be. It seemed a moveable end point, 'the end of the build', an almost mythical place you arrived at only when you had no wish to go any further. But the clunk of that last bolt sliding into the last bolthole had a certain finality to it.

So I called it, said out loud to no one but the currawongs calling in the evening, 'This is it, birds. After eight months of building and four months of tinkering, almost exactly a year since we started laying the floor joists across my steel trailer, my little house is finally... finished.'

It was the quietest milestone of the build. And it was fitting, somehow, that I was alone for it. This had always been my build, my 'crooked, winding, lonesome, dangerous' trail to walk, or stumble along, even when I hadn't been alone. There'd be a housewarming party later, to thank everyone who had worked on the tiny and share the 'We did it!' feeling, but this afternoon was just for me. And we *were* still in lockdown.

I packed away my tools and went inside. Then I made a pot of tea and put two squares of chocolate fudge on a small plate and I sat at my timber bench with the gas-strut window open, looking out at the trees.

# Epilogue

*'The way of love is not a subtle argument. The door there is devastation.
Birds make great sky circles of their freedom. How do they learn it?
They fall and falling, they're given wings.'* ~ Rumi

It's two years later and I'm sitting at my kitchen bench with a cup of tea again and all the windows open. The day is warm and it's late afternoon and in the pauses between thoughts I'm watching sunbeams slicing through the trees, listening to the rainbow lorikeets screeching somewhere far above me. Skinks skitter across sun-warmed rocks in my small garden. And there are flowers everywhere, stepping into the springtime spotlight: royal purple tibouchinas, daisy-like cosmoses, bridal gardenias. Peace lilies, too, unfurling their spinnaker petals and dancing in the breeze on long green stalks around my outdoor shower. They'd nodded at me as I'd stood out there this morning, rinsing off the salt after a swim in the sea. I'd nodded back.

This is my life now, but it took a little while for it to be like this.

⌂

Of all the things I learned during the build and its aftermath, one stands out: a home is not a promise of stability. And even if it were, it's a promise that's seldom kept. Because life is, still, life. Swirling around you, sometimes cradling you in its arms, sometimes smashing you to pieces, sometimes catching its breath and letting you do the same. And I was still me: sensitive, wanting to love and be loved, endlessly wondering.

When the build officially finished, when everything stopped, I was enveloped by grief and an unrelenting sadness the way dust engulfs a car that has skidded to a halt on an outback road. It surprised me. I'd watched a new kind of confidence grow in me during the build. I'd felt physically strong and mentally capable. I'd learned so much, about building, about relationships, about how interconnected everything is. I'd learned what drives me, about the wounds I carry, how to take care of myself. I'd loved making things with my hands. Inhabiting my body in a new way, I'd stepped into a simpler way of being – and working – even before I moved into my little house.

But in the immediate aftermath, I felt different. Not just heartbroken but broken in other ways. My self-confidence evaporated; I felt unsure of myself around other people. The pandemic probably played a role – didn't we all have a little social anxiety after two years of global uncertainty? – and the fact that I'd just emerged from an all-consuming project. I missed having a sense of purpose. It was natural to feel a little lost, I told myself. I'd let go of one trapeze and hadn't yet grabbed hold of another.

Part of me felt embarrassed because finishing the tiny was supposed to make me happier and my life better. Instead I wasn't quite sure what to do with myself and I was still living on Max's land (tiny house sites being hard to come by), like a stone stuck in the middle of a river while life flowed on around me, without me.

Then Max went away for five months, to help on a friend's building project in Tasmania. As soon as he left, a calm descended. I started writing this book, just for myself at first, to make sense of everything that had happened. I felt my soul creep back to me. And as it did, the tiny reminded me every day who I was, what was important to me, what I was capable of, and that everything would be all right.

Of course Max was all around me even when he wasn't here. Our story was in every floorboard and architrave. Things we'd once talked about doing together – watching movies in my day loft, snuggling in my bed during thunderstorms, making pancakes and pizzas at my kitchen bench – I was doing alone. But, increasingly, that felt OK. I was keeping myself company with these simple pleasures.

One day a friend asked me if it was hard to live in the home Max and I had built together, after all that had happened. It really wasn't. The tiny was still mine, still me, and as I started to feel more content I made space for a clear-eyed gratitude to him, untainted by our hard times, for all he'd done to help me. This had been our labour of love. That's what I saw – and still see – looking around at everything we'd made.

Building this little house took everything I had, on every level, in every way. I don't know whether it made me stronger or just gave me an opportunity to see how strong I could be, the way any adventure does. It made me softer, too, as hard things often do.

And in losing love, I found a new way to be. That was the trade-off. I couldn't have both, not with Max, I could see that now; I could be with him or with myself. So I made the only choice I could make. After choosing to stay at the start, I chose freedom at the end, but it wasn't the kind of freedom I'd had as a professional nomad. This was borne of something deeper, something I think I'd been searching for all my life, an ancient sense of belonging and safety, wherever I was. I'd had a taste of it when travel had helped me feel at home in the world; now my little house had brought me full circle, and home to myself.

Max and I eventually relaxed into the kind of friendliness you can have only with someone you've been through difficult times with. We never spoke of those times again. When he visits the tiny now, we marvel at what we created together.

And I found peace, or it found me. I found a beautiful new place to park the tiny: a quiet spot surrounded by trees, close to the sea. And I found my cabin-like existence, one that suited me in all the important ways: a simple life, close to nature, in a very small house.

⌂

Darkness has wrapped a silent blanket around the tiny. Soon I'll climb the stairs to my bed, where I might read for a while, listening to the low drumbeat of the surf through the open windows. Then I'll turn off the light and lie looking out, at the stars and the sliver of a new moon and the soundless shapes of the trees, until I fall asleep.

# Acknowledgements

Writing about building a tiny house is a lot more solitary than actually building a tiny house, but I couldn't have done it – or the build – without the support of some talented, wonderful people.

So many people helped out on the build, in so many ways, there's not enough space here to mention them all by name, but I hope they all know how much I appreciate every one of them. I'm especially, eternally, grateful to Max for, well, everything: his love, his great ideas, all his hard work and care, for letting me live on his land after the build until I found a new spot for the tiny, and so much else that made this such a big, life-changing adventure. A bow of thanks to George, too, for his hard work and aesthetic eye and for making sure my tiny would be structurally safe and sound. And to Wal for his gentle presence and steady paintbrush.

Thanks to my late mum, Elaine, for teaching me the true meaning of 'home' and for unwittingly sending me off on the adventure of my life, just over thirty years ago; and to Dad, for the financial support when funds ran low and for understanding that, even though tiny living isn't his style, I needed to do this. To Fred and Shannon Schultz of Fred's Tiny Houses, two people deeply committed to tiny living as a viable housing option, for the inspiring tiny-building courses, for my purpose-built trailer, for the Unified Construction Method and for their wise counsel along the way. And to Sophie Wilksch, my 'build-angel' from Shedding in Mullumbimby, for the woodworking course that taught me so much more than just how to make stuff.

Writing a memoir is such a strange thing to do, with all its soul-baring and thrashing around in the past, and on the days I wondered why I was doing it, my writer friends Christine Retschlag, Kerry Van Der Jagt, John Borthwick, Justine Costigan, Tom Neal Tacker, Angela Saurine and Anabel Dean reminded me. Big thanks to you all for the 'keep going!' messages, the encouraging phone calls and the thoughtful feedback on my uncertain early drafts. Thanks, too, to other friends who kindly read the manuscript and helped me make it better, including Shaun Eastment, Michele Eckersley, Katrina Lobley and Sean Tonnet (who deserves a special mention for being such an ally and the best psychotherapist a girl could have).

Thank you to the fantastic team at Hardie Grant Explore – particularly my publishers Megan Cuthbert, Danielle Dominguez and Melissa Kayser, editor Siboney Saavedra, publicist Marilla Marshall Sloan, designer Regina Abos and those working behind the scenes – for getting *Tiny* out into the world.

And thank *you* for silently urging me on from the other side of the page; I might have started writing it to process everything that happened, but this book was always for you.

Finally I'd like to acknowledge all the privileges and opportunities I've had throughout my life that led me to my tiny. I know tiny living isn't for everyone; I also know there are plenty of people for whom even a tiny house is out of reach. With the world deep in a housing crisis as well as climate, biodiversity and all sorts of other crises, the sooner governments at all levels legalise permanent living in tiny houses everywhere, not just in some places, the better.

## About the author

Louise Southerden is an author and award-winning travel writer who has spent more than twenty-five years travelling to faraway places, most recently for *The Sydney Morning Herald*, *The Age*, *Lonely Planet* and *MiNDFOOD*, specialising in sustainable, nature-based and regenerative travel. A keen swimmer and surfer, she's the author of four non-fiction titles including *Surf's Up*, the world's first women's guide to surfing, and *Japan: a working holiday guide*. Originally from Sydney, she now lives in her tiny house near the sea in northern NSW.

The quote from *Desert Solitaire* © 1988 by Edward Abbey, reprinted by permission of Don Congdon Associates, Inc.

Excerpt from *Tracks* by Robyn Davidson, copyright © 1980 by Robyn Davidson, reproduced with permission of Bloomsbury Publishing and Pantheon Books, an imprint of the Knopf Doubleday Publishing Group, a division of Penguin Random House LLC. All rights reserved.

Martin Buber quote from *The Legend of Baal-Shem* (1955), published by Princeton University Press, reproduced with permission from Roam Agency, representatives for the Estate of Martin Buber.

Richard R Powell quote reprinted from *Wabi Sabi Simple* by Richard R. Powell, ©2005 CWL Publishing Enterprises, Inc., with permission of the publisher. All rights reserved.

Martha Postlethwaite quote from *Addiction and Recovery: A Spiritual Pilgrimage* (2019) by Martha Postlewaite reproduced by permission of Fortress Press, an imprint of 1517 Media.

Quotes from *Hysterical* copyright © Elissa Bassist, 2022. Reprinted by permission of Elissa Bassist.

Anna Funder quote from *Wifedom: Mrs Orwell's Invisible Life* (2023) reprinted with permission from Penguin Random House Australia.

Every effort has been made to contact the copyright holders for materials used in this book and to obtain their permission. For any omissions, please contact the publisher directly and they will be corrected in future reprints and editions.